UNSHAKEABLE LOVE: A COUPLES GUIDE TO WINNING OVER BETRAYAL AND INFIDELITY

GET BACK THE TRUST AND SEXUAL INTIMACY IN YOUR RELATIONSHIP OR MARRIAGE

FRANK PARKER

CONTENTS

INTRODUCTION

"Healing does not mean the damage never existed. It means the damage no longer controls our lives."

— UNKNOWN

"I'm sorry." My wife could barely look at me through her tears. "I don't know how it happened. It didn't mean anything."

I didn't know what to say. I was numb, stunned at the news that my wife had been having an affair. She said it hadn't gone on for long and was more emotional than anything else, but in many ways, that was worse. Why had she turned to another man?

"It's over, I promise," my wife continued. "I really want to work things out with you. Can you give me a second chance?"

It was the hardest question I'd ever been asked, and, in that moment, I didn't have the answer.

On average, men are more likely to cheat than women. Studies show that, on average, 20% of men and 13% of women report having intercourse with someone other than their spouse.[1] However, the younger the couple, the narrower the gap—among married couples aged 18–29, 11% of women cheat, as compared to 10% of men. But as couples age, this changes dramatically until 24% of men in their 80s admit to cheating while only 6% of women stray.

Of course, these statistics may only reflect the tip of the iceberg. They come from those who *admit* to having an affair. Who knows how many more have cheated on their partner? Regardless of who cheated, the sad truth is that 40% of marriages end after an affair, regardless of who strayed, whereas only 17% of faithful married couples divorce.

And that was the dilemma I was facing. Did I want to be part of the 40%, or did I want to work things through?

Heather and I had been together since high school, and we had two children together. Whatever decision I made would impact them too. I dreaded the thought of sitting them down to tell them mommy had cheated on me, and we were splitting up. Who would get custody? Would Heather need to stay in the family home for the kids, or would she move out?

My mind was awhirl with dilemmas I never thought I'd have to face. But I didn't have to. It was my choice. If I worked things out with her, we'd never have to tell our children. We could still build a life together, a *new* life, one built on stronger foundations. We had an opportunity to create something special, but it would take both of us to be fully committed. I made my decision.

"I don't know if I'll ever forgive you," I told my wife. "But I'd like to try."

I had no idea how life-changing that moment would turn out to be. It's what set me on the course to qualify as a marriage counselor specializing in infidelity. My personal experience made me determined to help other couples navigate the stormy waters of a cheating spouse and either ride it out or realize the time has come to call it quits. But there were other effects.

My self-esteem hit rock bottom. I wondered what I'd done to deserve being treated like that, what was wrong with me that she turned to another man. I started to doubt myself and my judgment. Why hadn't I noticed something was wrong? Heather's affair didn't just shatter my trust in her—it made me wonder whether I could trust myself.

I went through a very dark time. I was hurt, angry, and bitter, and it came out in the way I interacted with the people around me, not just Heather. I was short with the children, and my friends commented that I didn't seem to be myself anymore. I realized that if I wanted to work things out with Heather, I needed to sort myself out as well as our relationship.

The reality is that while discovering your partner has had an affair can be one of the worst things ever to happen to you, it also can be a very positive opportunity.

For me, my wife's affair is what put me on the path to doing the work I do now, work I find incredibly rewarding. It helped me figure out what I did and didn't want from life. Much as I wish my wife hadn't felt the need to turn to another man, that was her choice. While I wouldn't have made the same choice if I'd been feeling the way she'd been feeling, ultimately, she was the one who would have to live with what she'd done. I couldn't control her thoughts or actions. All I could do was focus on my own thoughts and actions.

I spent a lot of time thinking about what I wanted to do, and I knew that even though it would be hard, I wanted to make my marriage work. It was going to be tough, and maybe we'd still go our own ways in the end, but if we could get through this, we'd be closer than ever.

We found a relationship therapist we both liked and started seeing him, together and separately. During this time, we were forced to dig deep into our goals and motivations. Did we still want the same things? Did we still share the same values?

Fortunately for our relationship, we did. Heather's guilt over her affair made her more motivated than ever to make it up to me, but I didn't want someone to stay with me because they felt they had to. I wanted her to stay because she loved me and wanted to build a future with me.

We spent many hours talking to each other and our therapist about our expectations and standards. While Heather had chosen to have an affair, I had to look at my own behavior and what I could do differently to make sure Heather didn't feel she had to go to someone else to have her needs fulfilled.

We talked about our love languages, what we do to express our love and what we needed from each other to feel loved. What our nonnegotiables were. How responsive we were to each other's needs and concerns.

I'm not going to pretend it was easy. It wasn't. There were some very dark times in the months following Heather's affair. But we both felt that what we had was worth pushing through. I still loved my wife, and looking back over our relationship, there were still more good times than bad.

This book is an accumulation of my personal experiences in coping with the aftermath of my wife's affair, combined with many years working as a professional counselor. Not only was forgiving my wife and choosing to stay in my marriage the right thing for me, but I've worked with many clients who have also found it was the right thing for them.

One client told me that forgiving her husband didn't mean that what he did was okay. It's just that she chose not to carry the burden of anger and resentment for the rest of her life. Another said it meant a lot that her husband had told her about the affair and actively asked for forgiveness instead of waiting for her to find out. He was open and honest when she asked questions about it and was happy to do whatever she wanted to keep their relationship going. She told me if she'd been the one to cheat, she would have wanted him to forgive her, so she decided to treat him the way she'd want to be treated. She insisted they get therapy together, which is how I ended up meeting them. They're still together, and their relationship is stronger than ever.

Every relationship is different. Every situation is different. My aim with this book is to give you the tools you need to navigate your way through the troubled waters you're currently in.

I'm not going to pretend it will be a walk in the park. It'll take hard work and commitment from both of you to get to the other side of this. But it *can* be done. I know because I've done it, and so have many of my clients. I'll be right by your side every step of the way. It's time to get to work.

Now, if you're going to move past betrayal successfully, the first step is to forgive. You may not be ready to do that right now, and that's okay. Everyone gets to that place in their own time.

Ask yourself:

- **Do I still resent my partner, or do I just feel sad about the situation?** It's normal for your initial response to be resentment, anger, or bitterness. But over time, this fades to be replaced by sadness. This is when you start to question whether you can forgive your partner, which brings you close to freeing yourself from the pain of the situation.
- **Do I want to let the past be the past?** Forgiveness allows us to let go of the emotional baggage we've been burdened with when we were betrayed. It is the key to freeing yourself from the shackles of negativity, allowing you to open up your heart again.
- **Do I want to stay with my partner?** It's natural to want to cut someone off when they betray us, but when faced with that reality, you may feel you still want them in your life. While missing someone isn't a good enough reason to take them back after an affair, if their presence in your life brings more happiness than it does sadness, you have good reason to choose to stay with them—or at least try to make it work before going your separate ways.
- **Can I set new boundaries?** When you forgive someone, you'll need to set new boundaries with them if you're going to continue to be together, so

> they don't hurt you again. Your relationship dynamic is going to have to change if you want things to be different in the future. If you feel capable of discussing, establishing, and maintaining new boundaries, it's a good sign that you're ready to forgive.

Above all, whatever the reason your partner cheated on you, *it's not your fault.* They didn't have to handle the situation in the way they did. Absolve yourself of any blame and understand that obsessing over the past and what might have been isn't going to help anyone. It's time to move forward and build a brighter future.

I want to clarify one thing: this book isn't intended to replace help from a professional therapist. If you've been the victim of infidelity, or you're the one who's cheated, this book is designed to support your worth through that experience while seeking help from a qualified therapist who will be able to support you through your individual circumstance. This will help make the healing process faster and more effective. They will also be able to assist you in tailoring the advice in this book for even better results.

Read on if you're ready to learn how to move past betrayal and build a stronger marriage than ever before. I've got everything you need to enjoy the loving, respectful relationship you truly deserve.

1

UNDERSTANDING BETRAYAL

As a counselor, I've heard many tragic and difficult stories over the years. I remember one client coming to me not long after she'd broken up with her boyfriend. She told me that she'd skipped work so she could organize a surprise party for her ex. She'd gone out of her way to invite all his friends, going through his social media to make sure that everyone he knew would be there.

Unfortunately, she had no idea that one of the people she invited was an ex-girlfriend. An ex-girlfriend it turned out he still had feelings for. The pair of them ended up hooking up at the party, not caring who saw them.

To make matters worse, when my client returned to work, she got fired for her unauthorized absence.

There was another client who had just found out her husband was cheating. She'd recently given birth to their first baby and had needed to take a month off sex to let her body recover. Her husband apparently didn't want to wait a month to have his needs fulfilled, so he downloaded Tinder and went on a number of dates. The only reason she found out was because one of her friends came across his Tinder profile.

The first client split up with her partner and is now happily married to someone else. Believe it or not, the second client managed to work things through with her husband, and they've had two more babies—this time without any cheating!

Infidelity can happen to anyone, and it's never the fault of the person being cheated on—whatever they might want to say. If you're unhappy in a relationship, there are many other things you can do to change your situation that don't involve sleeping with someone else.

WHAT'S A NORMAL REACTION TO DISCOVERING INFIDELITY?

Being cheated on is one of the most painful experiences for anyone. It doesn't matter if the affair was recent or happened a long time ago and has only just come to light. It *hurts* to know you've been betrayed.

People often ask me, "Is how I'm feeling normal?" The truth is that there are a number of reactions to infidelity, and every single one is 'normal.' For many, learning your loved one is cheating on you triggers a physical response. The nervous system comes online, forcing a powerful response that can return whenever we're confronted with a reminder of the affair, making us feel like we're learning about it for the first time all over again.

Since the nervous system is involved, you may be in a continual state of 'fight, flight, or freeze.'

- **Fight.** Many people who've suffered infidelity find themselves becoming angry and irritable. After all, they've been betrayed in the worst possible way. They thought they could trust the foundations of their relationship, and instead, it feels like any shared values are a dim and distant memory. This can result in an explosive outburst of anger or a constant stream of anger and aggression. Alternatively, they may constantly ask their partner questions or demand in-depth knowledge about them. While this behavior is totally normal, it's not a healthy or sustainable way to be in a relationship. Your anger may be totally justified; letting that anger spill into physical or emotional abuse is not. Interrogating your partner is not going to build trust. Letting anger rule you for too long will leave you and your partner emotionally exhausted, and it will be difficult to rebuild your connection.

- **Flight.** Some people leave the moment they discover about an affair. Again, this is perfectly normal and natural. For some, this departure is for good. For others, it's a much-needed time to process and make sense of their experience. However, letting this break go on for too long will make it difficult for you to work through it together. What might have started as a temporary pause for breath becomes permanent, even when that wasn't what you wanted.
- **Freeze.** You may feel emotionally numb when you discover you've been cheated on. This can be easier than dealing with the pain directly. This response may take many different forms—you might bury yourself in work, spend hours playing video games, or start making plans for what life is going to be like without your partner while still maintaining the relationship in the meantime. Blocking out the pain might seem like the easy option, but until you face up to it, you won't be able to deal with it and ultimately move past it.

There are also common reactions from the cheater, who will be facing their own challenges:

- **Defensiveness.** Some unfaithful spouses find themselves trying to defend what they've done, whether it be the affair itself or the behavior surrounding the affair. It can be challenging to face up to how you've negatively affected someone else, and being expected to constantly prove or explain yourself can lead to defensiveness or even resentment.

- **Impatience.** This is probably the most frequent reaction I see. Many unfaithful spouses just want to move on and find it hard to understand why their partner is still hung up on the affair. It is understandable that a cheating partner who has made a choice to recommit to the relationship would want to move on quickly, but there is still healing that needs to be done, and that takes time. In addition, it can be difficult to look at the reasons why someone cheated and what has to be done to repair and rebuild.
- **Grief.** This is one of the most complex reactions to an affair and possibly the hardest for the betrayed spouse to come to terms with. Affairs usually happen for a reason which can be because of a need that was not met in the relationship. So, someone may be grieving the loss of a relationship even while being committed to making their marriage work. It is important to accept this grief and allow time to process it.

SHAME

A common reaction for *both* parties is shame. Shame about having an affair and shame about being cheated on. In fact, I've observed that the overwhelming majority of couples choose to hide the fact of the affair, whether they actively agreed to do so or not. There seems to be a consensus that infidelity is embarrassing. What's more, while you might understand the cheater feeling embarrassed about what they've done, I've found that the faithful partner feels it all the more. There is a sense that they must be the ones who *really* did something wrong. It's their fault the marriage faltered. Of course, it isn't, but since when were emotions logical?

Another factor can be that the betrayed partner wants to keep things secret because they're afraid that if the truth came out, it would upset the cheater, who would end the relationship completely. Thus, neither partner feel able to be fully open, and trust becomes harder and harder to build.

For the person who cheated, it can be hard to accept that they behaved that way, especially if their self-image is one of integrity. They may not have planned to have an affair. It just happened.

Facing up to shame is incredibly important in overcoming it. Ignoring any emotional emotions doesn't make them go away. In fact, it only creates more problems. You may find yourself turning to negative coping methods, such as drinking, drugs, overeating, and even excessive exercise. Not only will these not tackle the shame, but they will also make you feel worse about yourself.

Find someone you can talk to about your shame. This can be a trusted friend or a therapist. Talking about your feelings without feeling judged will help you accept, process, and move past them.

WHAT IS INFIDELITY ANYWAY?

Infidelity may also be known as cheating or adultery. It is the act of being involved in emotional or sexual intimacy with someone outside of the agreed boundaries of your relationship. It does not have to involve sexual activity and may take place in person or online.

It can be difficult to be sure your partner is cheating on you without having direct evidence. However, there are usually some red flags that will give you a sign of what's going on. These may include:

- Your partner is less interested in sex.
- Your partner may want you to be involved in sexual acts which you find foreign or off-putting.
- Your partner takes extra care over their appearance.
- Your partner may be having difficulties sleeping.
- Your partner may appear distracted or stressed.
- Your partner may demand more privacy than usual.

- Your partner may want to spend more time alone or be away from home more often.
- Your partner may be more hostile or aggressive than usual.
- You may find yourself suffering from insomnia, stress, or distraction because you're suspicious of your partner.

Believe it or not, there are eleven different types of infidelity:

1. **Conflict avoidance affairs.** When a partner actively seeks to avoid any kind of conflict, they may have an affair to meet their needs which cannot be expressed to their spouse. These affairs usually don't last long but may recur many times.
2. **Intimacy avoidance affairs.** When someone is afraid of intimacy, they may use an affair to keep an emotional distance between themselves and their spouse. As with conflict avoidance affairs, they tend not to last long but often are repeated. However, if both partners are intimacy avoiders, affairs like these may help them maintain an emotionally distant relationship.
3. **Individual/existential/developmental-based affairs. Midlife crises,** empty nest syndrome, depression, or a general sense of emptiness can all be triggers for an affair. The affected partner may take a lover to rediscover themselves or cope with anxiety,

depression, or other negative feelings arising from the stress of dealing with the aging process or a lack of spiritual fulfillment. An affair may be their way of feeling attractive again or wanting to fulfill certain desires or fantasies rather than any dissatisfaction with the marriage itself.

4. **Sexual addiction affairs.** Sex addicts have poor impulse control, using sex to mask their inner pain and angst. They are drawn to the buzz of an orgasm but then have to deal with the come down into shame and worthlessness.
5. **Accidental-brief affairs.** This is the kind of affair that 'just happens' because someone is in the wrong place at the right time. It is unplanned and may occur due to curiosity, pity, drunkenness, etc., resulting in a brief and usually one-off affair.
6. **Philandering.** Some people are more likely to cheat, whether because of insecurity, low self-esteem, or a need for external validation. Narcissistic and impulsive individuals are particularly likely to engage in this type of affair. Philanderers view extramarital sex as something they're entitled to and will be happy to take advantage of any opportunities presenting themselves without feeling any guilt about it.
7. **Retribution affairs.** These arise because one partner feels like they need to get revenge on the other. There may be many reasons for this—it might be the

other partner cheated, or has withheld money, love, or emotion, or they may have done something else the partner felt was an injustice.

8. **Bad marriage affairs.** These come about because a marriage suffers from poor communication or a lack of intimacy and/or support. There may also be factors involving incompatible cultural and familial values. When a marriage is unhappy, one or both partners may look for a solution in an extramarital affair.
9. **Exit affairs.** These are used as an excuse to end a marriage, whether planned or not. They often result in a partner having a new relationship in place before leaving the marriage, so they don't have to be alone.
10. **Parallel lives affairs.** These are long-term affairs with a second partner. The other spouse may be aware of such an affair and tolerate it without ever directly addressing it.
11. **Online affairs.** These are becoming increasingly prevalent due to the accessible, affordable, and anonymous nature of the internet. They may involve watching someone online via video, talking on instant messenger services, in chatrooms, or via email or telephone. They can occur at any time of the day or night and even in the family home while the other spouse is around. The lack of physical contact

during a sex act can often make the relationship even more intense.

THE IMPACT OF INFIDELITY

The pain caused by infidelity can be overwhelming. You may feel grief for the relationship you thought you had, anger for being betrayed, or sadness for the loss of all your hopes and dreams. The impact can be so devastating that Dr. Dennis Ortman described it as a form of trauma, calling it 'Post-Infidelity Stress Disorder,'[1] claiming that the phases of recovery from the trauma of infidelity are akin to the five stages of grief. Research also shows that infidelity can induce increased levels of anxiety, depression, and stress.[2]

However, you're feeling is absolutely valid. Let your experience be your experience.

THE LONG-TERM IMPACT OF BEING CHEATED ON

It can take a long time to recover from an affair. When we are in love, the emotion triggers the release of oxytocin and dopamine, hormones responsible for making us feel good. This can be addictive to the brain, so when you feel rejected because your partner had an affair, it can cause changes in the structure of the brain, which are similar to the impact of recovering from substance abuse.[3] You may experience similar symptoms to PTSD, such as flashbacks, nightmares, and obsessing over what happened. You may become overly reactive to any perceived threats, either to yourself or your relationship, and your sleeping and eating patterns may be disturbed.

If you have children, they will also be affected if they discover one of their parents cheated. They may decide to side with the wronged spouse, trusting them more. They may feel similar emotions to the betrayed spouse, such as confusion, anxiety, abandonment, and isolation. They may struggle to trust their own future romantic partners and have negative ideas around fidelity.

There is good news, however. It is possible to heal and move on from an affair. Our brains have an ability to learn new skills, known as neuroplasticity.

One study examined how the brain responds and adapts to trustworthy social encounters versus untrustworthy ones.[4] This teaches us who we can and can't trust.

Using MRI scans, researchers discovered that when we experience unexpected cooperation from another person, we change our behavior more than when we are unexpectedly betrayed. The more social encounters we have, the less our brain responds to untrustworthy people.

So the more we deal with untrustworthy people, the less surprised we are by it, but the less we react to it. Conversely, the more we surround ourselves with trustworthy people, the more we appreciate it and engage in pro-social behavior.

We naturally tend to focus on those we can trust, which will protect us from being betrayed.

This means that our brain adjusts with every experience so that we can move toward surrounding ourselves with more and more trustworthy people so we aren't betrayed again. This also means that it's natural to feel wary of your partner following an affair. It will take time for those original pathways to be rebuilt.

WHY DO PEOPLE CHEAT IN THE FIRST PLACE?

There are many, many different reasons why someone might cheat:

- **They may be naturally predisposed.** One form of personality test measures how someone ranks for agreeableness, conscientiousness, openness, extraversion and neuroticism, known as the Big Five. When an individual scores low for both agreeableness and conscientiousness, they're more likely to cheat.
- **Your lives are separated.** If you're not sharing meaningful aspects of your lives, one partner may be more likely to cheat. If you are reserved and distant from your partner, it may result in one of you deciding to build a life with someone else.
- **You struggle to accept your differences.** While opposites may attract, they may also find it hard to

maintain a long-term relationship. While someone's differences might initially be attractive and a way of balancing you out, over time, those differences can drive a wedge between you as a pair.

- **One of you develops narcissistic traits.** All of us change as we age, whether that be for good or bad. If your partner develops narcissistic traits or starts to look for attention elsewhere, e.g., flirting with the server when you go out for a meal together, this can be a red flag for infidelity.

Three main categories detail why someone cheats: individual, relationship, and situational. Individual reasons mean someone has personality traits that make them more inclined to cheat. Religion, politics, and gender may also have an influence. Relationship reasons mean someone is feeling unhappy in their relationship for whatever reason. Situational reasons are those external influences that tempt someone to cheat when they wouldn't usually otherwise, e.g., starting a new job or moving home.

Within these categories are a number of other more detailed reasons:

- **You've fallen out of love.** Many cheaters say they strayed because either they didn't feel like they loved their partner, or they had stronger feelings for someone else.

- **You feel like a change.** Sometimes, people feel bored in their relationship, so they look for ways to spice things up. Or, they might be happy with their partner, but they want to explore different aspects of themselves. It's more about leaving the person they've become rather than the relationship itself.
- **You feel neglected.** If you're not getting the attention you need from your partner, you may decide to look for it elsewhere. This is a particularly common motive among women.
- **You were in a particular situation.** Not everyone plans to have an affair. Someone might find themselves in a difficult situation, such as having gone drinking or being with someone who makes a pass at them and for whatever reason, they reciprocate. This is more common among men.
- **You feel the need to boost your self-esteem or ego**. While the long-term impact of an affair can result in severe, negative consequences, in the moment, an affair can give someone a lift to their ego or self-esteem.
- **You feel angry with your partner.** You may have had an argument with a partner or been going through a rough patch and see an affair as a way of punishing them or getting revenge.
- **You don't feel committed to your partner.** If you don't feel like you're committed to being with your partner, you may decide to stray.

- **You want to fulfill sexual urges.** It may be that everything's great in your relationship except your sex life. Maybe you're not having as much sex as you like, or you want to engage in specific activities your partner won't, so you find someone else who will meet your sexual needs.
- **Your testosterone levels are high if you're male.** While hormones aren't an excuse for cheating, there is evidence to show that if a man's testosterone levels are high, he may feel more inclined to cheat. Studies have shown that men in committed relationships experience lower levels of testosterone and feel less inclined to cheat, while men with higher levels of testosterone are more interested in having sex with other people.[5]
- **You're ovulating if you're female.** Women are more likely to cheat when they are ovulating and more likely to get pregnant. Biologically, women seek out the men with the best genes to father their children. Men in high demand may not be faithful or stick around once the baby is born, so a woman in a committed relationship might feel the urge to cheat during the fertile part of her cycle to give her baby better genes. Again, this isn't an excuse to cheat, but it does provide a little insight into what might be going on in the body to drive certain behaviors.
- **You're a serial cheater.** There is a certain amount of truth to the saying, once a cheater, always a cheater.

> One study found that someone who had cheated in a relationship was three times more likely to cheat on their next partner.[6]

THE IMPORTANCE OF ADDRESSING BETRAYAL TRAUMA

We've already discussed the fact that betrayal can cause trauma. If you've decided you want to save your marriage (and if you're reading this book, you're at least considering it), it's vital you face up to your experience of post-infidelity trauma disorder.

You should first know that how you react to the knowledge that your partner has had an affair is hardwired into you. Human beings are biologically programmed to bond with their fellow humans by building deep, nurturing attachments, which means we're more inclined to look after and defend each other against attacks. If that bond is broken, it's naturally traumatizing.

Our nervous system is great at identifying a threat but not so good at determining what kind of threat. A betrayal is a very different threat to the prospect of being eaten by a tiger, but to your nervous system, it's all equally threatening. This is why your emotions may feel scattered when you discover your partner has been cheating on you, or you may not know what you feel—a clear sign of trauma.

If the impact of trauma is buried instead of addressed, it can lead to long-term problems, where you may feel paranoid or overreact to the smallest things. Given time, you may feel better, but those feelings haven't gone away; they've just been buried and are waiting to resurface when triggered.

Dealing with the trauma of an affair might be difficult, but in the long term, it's the healthiest thing to do.

WILL YOU EVER RECOVER FROM AN AFFAIR?

The short answer is yes, regardless of whether that's with your marriage intact or not. But if you want your marriage to last, I'm living proof that you *can* move past it to a brighter future.

Ideally, you should get support from a qualified therapist to help you through these difficult times. They will provide you with an impartial framework for you to explore your feelings and heal.

We're going to dive deeper into practical ways of dealing with betrayal later in this book, but for now, here are a few starting points for you to consider:

- **Trust your judgment.** If you have any worries, anything at all, say so. It doesn't matter whether you are correct in your assumptions or not. Right now, what matters more is that your spouse is willing to listen and respond to your concerns. If they're not, it raises questions over whether they're going to be able to give you the emotional support you need to get through this.

- **Don't minimize the affair.** If you're the one who cheated, it can be tempting to play things down in a bid to make your partner feel better. In fact, this frequently makes things worse because brushing off their fears can come across as if you've got more to hide.
- **Keep things on a need-to-know basis.** While you will need support to get through this, this is best sought from a professional or impartial friend who will hold space for you to decide what you want to do. If you tell everyone what's happened and then decide to stay with your spouse, this can do severe, or even irreparable, damage to your social network. Some of your friends may never forgive your partner, even if you do, which can make things difficult in the future. You may even lose friendships over it.
- **Make a decision.** If you're caught up in a choice between your spouse or your lover, decide whom you're going to stay with and end the other relationship. If not, what sometimes happens is that the spouse will go along with it because they're worried about being alone or you have children together. The problem with this is that it only prolongs the hurt. You have to both agree to work on

your relationship if you're going to stay together and then commit. It's the only way forward. And if you do decide to stay together, you have to accept that you'll never see your lover again.

- **Look at the bigger picture.** While the cheater is always the one to blame for the affair, it's always a good idea to consider the state of your relationship at this point. What issues do you have that need to be worked on? Did you start to take each other for granted or stop talking through your problems? Identifying existing issues doesn't excuse the affair, but it can give you a common ground to work on in the future.
- **Give it time.** It's going to take at least a year to recover from being betrayed. It requires consistency and regularly doing what you say you'll do and being where you say you'll be. Know that this stage won't last forever, and things will get better if you're both putting in the effort.
- **Focus on peace and closure.** Eventually, you're going to have to move past this. You can't punish the offender forever. Complete honesty is essential. Get as much information as you need about the affair to get closure. The unknown is scary, so discussing what happened and why allows you to get the information you need to process the situation and then start afresh. Let go of those aspects of your relationship which weren't working and treat this as

an opportunity to build a new dynamic in your relationship. Things can never be the same again, but that doesn't mean you can't still have a strong relationship together.

In this chapter, we've explored the subject of infidelity in great depth, so you know:

- The definition of infidelity.
- Reactions to infidelity.
- The long-term impact of infidelity.
- The reasons for infidelity.
- What you can do to start repairing and rebuilding your relationship.

While an affair can be devastating, if both of you are willing to do the hard work, it is possible to recover and even see the positive side of a difficult situation.

In the next chapter, we'll start this process by digging into the power of complete honesty.

2

COMPLETE HONESTY

"I think I can rebuild my marriage without ever telling Becky," John said in one of our sessions. "I've ended it with Christina, and I'm willing to do what it takes to make it up to Becky without her ever knowing."

"Do you?" I looked at John impassively, waiting for him to expand on it.

"I mean . . . I think . . . I want . . ." he stuttered and fell into silence.

"Any healthy relationship has to be built on honesty," I told him. "Maybe Becky doesn't suspect you had an affair, but she'll know something is wrong. I'm not going to tell you that you have to tell her right now, but I think you should consider whether you *really* can fix your marriage without telling her something this big."

As already discussed in the introduction, roughly 20% of married men and 13% of married women cheat. According to a survey carried out by Health Testing Centers,[1] just under half of the people questioned said they'd cheated in a relationship. Of those, half said they told their partner about the affair. Almost half told their partner within a week of cheating, while roughly a quarter confessed within a month, with the rest waiting six months or longer to come clean.

WHY DO PEOPLE CHOOSE TO LIE ABOUT AN AFFAIR?

In my sessions, I've heard every reason imaginable why someone doesn't want to tell their spouse about an affair. The most common include:

- *I've made my peace with God. Why should I tell my spouse?* While I respect and admire anyone with strong religious convictions, ultimately, you will still need to make things right with your partner. While dishonesty might not be a deadly sin, it's still not exactly behavior any God would condone.
- *I'd only be telling my partner to make myself feel better.* Really? Confessing to an affair is going to be an emotionally fraught conversation for both of you. It's not going to make either of you feel good in the short term. However, you need to consider whether you can really live with the guilt of what you've

done. Can you look at your spouse without thinking about the fact they're blissfully unaware you cheated? In the long term, that guilt will do more harm than good. While it's going to be upsetting for your partner to find out what's happened, overall, it will hurt you both less than keeping it secret.

- *What they don't know can't hurt them.* It's nice to think this is the case, but the reality is that secrets tend to impact our behavior, whether we're conscious of it or not. Your partner will suspect that something's wrong, and feeling like you are keeping something from them most definitely will hurt.
- *They'll leave me.* Yes, that's certainly possible. That's the risk you took when you decided to have an affair. But if you're serious about making your marriage work, you'll need to start with a clean slate and build on solid foundations. That means telling them everything and accepting that it could be the end of your relationship—or it could be the start of a stronger one.
- *My spouse really doesn't suspect a thing. We could just continue as we are, couldn't we?* Sure, you could. But that's not going to fix the problems which led to you having an affair, which means there's a chance you could do it again. A relationship needs to have complete honesty if it's going to be healthy and thrive. You need to talk about what happened and why.

- *They won't be able to deal with the truth.* Maybe. Again, that's the chance you took when you cheated. But maybe they'll surprise you. You have no idea what their reaction will be unless you talk to them about it.
- *It was just a fling. It'll never happen again.* Unfortunately, I've found that the people who tell themselves that are the ones who end up cheating again and again. You need to tackle the root causes that made you stray, and that's only going to happen if you talk it through with your spouse.
- *I just want to pretend it never happened.* I hear that. It's understandable to want to act as if your mistakes didn't happen. But they did. Sticking your head in the sand isn't going to let you resolve the problems in your marriage and won't support you in building a stronger relationship.
- *My spouse will never find out.* Maybe not. But maybe they will. You just can't know for certain. And if your spouse finds out from another source, the pain will be that much worse. Thinking you can get away with it is going to make you feel that you can cheat again, which means you'll only repeat your mistakes.

THE IMPACT OF DISHONESTY

For many people, while an affair was hurtful, the lies were the most damaging thing. When we discover we've been deceived, it shatters our trust in others as well as ourselves. We can no longer rely on our perceptions and opinions. We feel like we don't know our partner at all. There's a whole different side to them we did not know about.

Compromise is an essential part of a relationship. The problem is that many of us compromise ourselves in order to make someone else happy. We enter into new relationships burdened with the baggage of our past, making it difficult to stop negative habits and patterns of behavior we developed to deal with past situations. This then impacts how we interact with our partners. Maybe we become jealous or possessive because we've been cheated on in the past, but this then makes us try to control our partner, who then becomes more likely to have an affair, not less. Or we don't speak up about things that are upsetting us, so the problem gets bigger and bigger. Both of you pretend everything's okay, but one or both of you will start to resent the other, and the relationship will start to fall apart.

When we act with integrity and are honest about ourselves, we don't have to compromise or act out of any sense of guilt or obligation. What's more, we aren't inadvertently pushing our partner to compromise themselves either. The more open and honest a couple is with each other, the healthier and more resilient the relationship is. Conversely, the more lies, deceptions, and secrets are normalized, the more likely we will get comfortable with bigger and bigger lies.

When you have an affair, lying about it may help maintain the illusion that everything's okay when it isn't. Your partner deserves to know that something's wrong, so they have a chance to put it right. They need to know they can believe what you tell them. If lies enter into the equation, it's only a matter of time before everything falls apart.

BEING HONEST AFTER AN AFFAIR

It might feel like it's impossible to start again from a place of honesty after you've lied and cheated or been lied to and cheated on, but it isn't. It will take work and time, but it is possible to get back into a place of trust. The strongest relationships are built on a foundation of honesty and transparency. Imagine being able to be with your partner, knowing that they love and accept you, even with all your flaws and faults. What greater proof of love could there be?

When you tell your spouse you've had an affair, it can be difficult to know how much detail to go into. You might want to gloss over what happened or not want to talk about it because you're trying to put it in the past.

If you're the one who've been cheated on, it's a different story. While your partner has obviously known about their affair, it's news to you, so you'll have a lot of questions. It's very normal for you to have a lot of questions and want to know every little detail..

This is the time to be completely honest—cards on the table time. Unless there is a risk of physical abuse or suicide, answer any and all questions without prevarication. Trust can only be rebuilt if you're honest from this moment forward.

This can be harder for some than others. Many of us are used to hiding our feelings, believing that being vulnerable is a weakness and we don't want to be exposed. This may come from a place of feeling that if our partner knows our weaknesses, not only will they never trust us again, but they also won't love us.

The paradox here is that if you can't be honest, you can't be loved for who you are. It's time to try a new way to get the loving, trusting relationship you want and deserve.

You'll need to prove you are worthy of trust. This might involve doing some difficult things, such as giving your partner access to your social media accounts and devices or letting them track you via your phone. You might promise to answer your phone whenever they call and put it on speaker if you're in a situation where you genuinely can't talk, so they can hear you're telling the truth. Whatever strategies you put in place are for you to decide on but be prepared to take action rather than simply promising you'll be honest in future.

HOW IMPORTANT IS FULL DISCLOSURE?

If you're going to rebuild your relationship after an affair, you're going to need to rebuild trust, which by default means you have to be honest from here on forward. The big question is just how honest you should be and unfortunately, the jury's out on that one.

Personally, I recommend navigating this process with the support of a qualified therapist you're both comfortable with. While the cheated spouse deserves the answers to whatever questions they have, you also need to think about whether certain information is truly valuable or whether it's going to cause even more harm. For example, I had one client who demanded her partner tell her in great detail about every single sex act and then refuse to engage in the same acts ever again. Unsurprisingly, that relationship ended up in the divorce courts.

Then there have been occasions where the cheater has been open and honest about everything they did, sharing the details so they could save their marriage, only to have their partner's divorce lawyer use all that information against them.

It's a very tricky line to walk.

Each couple is different and the amount of detail required will depend on a range of factors, including whether there's any potential for violence, any mental health problems, your social or religious background, and personality type. This is why I work with couples on an individual basis to determine the best approach for them.

One way to deal with the situation is for the cheater to put together a disclosure document with the help of their therapist to give their spouse all the information about what happened. The wronged party can come up with a list of questions about what they've learned, again with the help of their therapist, who can help them determine whether a question is essential or whether it's likely to cause more harm.

For example, asking, "Did you risk my health?" is very important, especially since a lot of people having extramarital sex don't use protection. On the other hand, asking for intimate details about what exactly went on in the bedroom is unlikely to serve any real purpose unless there were existing sexual problems in the relationship.

For some people, giving too much information could do more harm than good. For others, too little will only leave them obsessing over what they don't know.

When you are telling your spouse about your affair, be considerate of their feelings and show remorse. Don't focus on how much fun it was and how much you enjoyed being with the other person. Be direct. This is going to hurt. There's no getting around that. Be prepared to answer whatever questions your spouse has, and remember that at this stage, the future of your relationship all hinges on how the cheating partner handles things. Avoid being defensive and try to stay as factual as you can. Finally, apologize unconditionally without expecting or demanding forgiveness at this point. That will come when the time is right.

If you are the one who was cheated on, try to be strong as you listen and attempt to understand what you're hearing. Try not to go on the attack or look at this process as an opportunity to punish your partner for what they've done to you. Talk everything through. If you're serious about staying together, try to keep an open mind. You will get past this. Understanding what happened to get you into this mess will help you prevent it from happening in the future. Both of you will likely need to make changes, but in the long term, this will make you both happier and avoid any need to cheat again.

When you've worked through the questions in therapy, you can then draw a line under what happened and work toward what you're going to do differently in the future. While it's likely that other questions may arise in the future—which should always be answered—when you've worked through the experience with a therapist, you can put your focus on where it's supposed to be—your relationship rather than an affair.

Sharing the story of the affair stops the wronged party from turning private investigator. If they have all the details they need, they can grieve what happened and then begin to pick up the pieces. This is the first step toward healing and saving the marriage.

THE OBSESSION CYCLE

It is very common for someone who has been cheated on to fall into what's known as the obsession cycle. This is when they feel hurt by what's happened, so they ask questions they've asked previously, needing new details. When they don't get a satisfactory answer, they get angry or upset and withdraw. Their obsession builds until their hurt becomes overwhelming, and the cycle starts all over again.

If you find yourself asking the same questions repeatedly, you're caught up in the obsession cycle. It's natural to think that more information will help heal the pain, and sometimes it will. But if it goes on too long, it becomes a way of you avoiding actively processing your hurt and looking deeper into what you need to do to rebuild your relationship.

I find that journaling really helps with this process. You can look over it and notice if there are any recurring themes. Once you've identified them, ask yourself if you knew all the answers, would it actually change anything? Would it help you process your feelings so you could move on?

Maybe, maybe not.

Using your journal to write out your anger and grief means you aren't constantly bombarding your partner with the same questions, which will eventually lead to resentment. You'll be able to start processing what's happened and will have a record you can look over to see how you've changed and notice that you have progressed, even if it doesn't feel like it.

THE DEPRESSION CYCLE

Another potential pitfall is the depression cycle. It's natural to feel depressed when you're dealing with the aftermath of being cheated on. This leads to you feeling sorry for yourself, as you notice how the affair has negatively impacted you. But then you start to feel sorry for your partner, as you see how they're struggling with the impact of their affair. This leads to you feeling angry with yourself for feeling sorry for someone who's hurt you so badly, which brings you back to depression.

When you've been cheated on, you can find yourself cycling through all sorts of emotions. You think about yourself, how hard done by you are, how unfair it all is, and how angry you are with your spouse. But then you think about them. You start to see their side of the story. You look for excuses for their behavior and think of ways to justify their behavior. This cycle continues, taking you on a real rollercoaster of emotions.

These feelings and thoughts are a natural part of processing what's happened. But some people get stuck here and can't seem to break free.

You might get stuck in the anger part of the process, which will result in bitterness and resentment. If anything happens in the future to trigger memories of what's happened, that anger will come flooding back. It can result in unwanted behavior, which can be highly self-destructive.

Alternatively, you might get stuck on the other side of the cycle, looking for reasons to excuse away what happened. This can lead to you shutting down your emotions or feeling depressed. When you put a wall up between yourself and those around you, you can't find your way back to the love you once shared. You feel even more depressed, and the impact on your relationship makes things worse.

Allow yourself to feel angry and sad. This is the only way to process your emotions and move past them. However, don't let these emotions be an excuse to treat your partner badly. Talk about your feelings rather than bottle them up, even if they don't seem to make sense. You feel how you feel, and that's okay. Try to empathize with your spouse. You'll both have feelings about what happened, and they'll probably be more similar than you realize. Reconnecting will allow you to work through them together.

A GUIDE TO COMPLETE HONESTY

Earlier in this chapter, we touched upon disclosing the details of your affair to your spouse. Doing this the right way demonstrates that you regret what happened and are committed to putting in the effort to heal your relationship. This is the time to put your spouse's needs before your own, but you'll need to do it right if you're going to be able to move forward.

- **Write it down.** When you first start discussing what happened, emotions are going to be running high. Writing it out allows you to take a step back, consider exactly how you want to explain things and consider how much detail to include. You can also take your time over the document to make sure you've remembered everything important.
- Having a written document enables your spouse to get a clear picture of what happened, and they can go over it again if they need to get details they may have missed the first time around. It also allows you to focus on the issue at hand rather than getting side-tracked in the heat of the moment.
- **Keep the focus on your own behavior/actions.** Write about what happened, where, when, and with whom. Don't get caught up in emotions or flowery descriptions.

- **Share your thoughts and motivations.** It's important to be honest about how you justified your affair to yourself without passing the blame to your spouse. Ultimately, you chose to have an affair when you could have made different choices. The responsibility is still yours. But you could write something like: "I was feeling . . . but I realize now that was no excuse."
- **Share your emotions.** It's easy to think your spouse isn't interested in your feelings and that the best thing you can do is listen to them talk about theirs. In fact, both your feelings are valid and important. When you share how you feel, you're opening up and being vulnerable, which is just what your partner needs when they're feeling vulnerable themselves.
- **Write about how your infidelity has affected you and those around you.** When you're caught up in an affair, you're rarely thinking about how it's going to impact those around you. If you did, you probably wouldn't have had an affair in the first place. At the very least, it would have taken away some of the fun and excitement. Now is the time to reflect on the extent of the damage you've done.
- **Strive for the right amount of detail.** Too much information is overwhelming and can be hurtful. Too little can make it seem like you're still trying to hide something. Consider writing something like this:

We met for the first time while you had taken the kids to visit your parents for the weekend. We went to a local hotel because it felt wrong to bring her back to our home. She booked and paid for a room at the motel down the road from my office. After you left, I called her to get the details of our room and drove to the hotel. We had unprotected sex. I decided not to spend the night because it felt too intimate. As soon as it was over, I regretted it.

THE DOS AND DON'TS OF CONFESSING TO AN AFFAIR

- **Do work with a therapist.** This is going to be the most effective way of helping you both cope with all the strong emotions you'll be experiencing to find a way forward.
- **Don't feel you have to know all the details right away.** While you might feel like you want to know everything the second you find out, it might not be the best time to get the answer to all your questions. Given time, you might find you don't need or want to know everything.
- **Do share an appropriate amount of detail.** As we've just discussed, too much or too little information can be damaging. Sharing intimate, graphic details might be impossible to move past. Discuss with a therapist first if you're unsure whether you should talk about something.

- **Don't feel like you have to make a decision right now.** When you find out about an affair, the future can seem uncertain. Know that you don't have to decide anything right away. We rarely make good decisions when we're feeling overwhelmed. Take the time to think about it, discuss the situation with a few trusted people, and consider your options.
- **Do tell the truth.** It's normal to want to lie after an affair has been discovered, either overtly or by omission. When someone is panicked and doesn't want to lose their spouse, it's natural to leave out certain things or lie because they're afraid of the consequences. Trust me. Things won't get any worse but lying about it will definitely make it worse.
- **Don't drip feed information.** Make sure you tell your spouse all the important details upfront. Telling them a part of the story, then a few days later revealing a little more and then a little more a few days after that will leave your spouse feeling insecure and on edge, waiting for the next bit of bad news. This is why a disclosure document written with the guidance of a therapist can be so valuable. It gets everything out in the open right from the start.
- **Do choose the right time and place to disclose your affair.** Ideally, the best way to deal with the full disclosure of an affair is with the assistance of a qualified counselor. If this isn't possible, consider

carefully when and where would be the most appropriate.

- **Don't discuss the details:**

  - In front of children.
  - While under the influence of alcohol or drugs.
  - Late at night.
  - In public (such as at work, over social media, at church, etc.).
  - Via text, email, or phone.
  - In a car.

EXERCISES

These are a few exercises you can do with your spouse to start the process of working through infidelity. Ideally, find a therapist to support you through these exercises, but if this isn't possible for whatever reason, find an appropriate time and place to do them so you can work through them at your own pace.

The Honesty after an Affair Exercise

1. Create a list of questions

Write down every single thing you've been wanting to ask your spouse about their affair. Then go over each question and ask yourself whether you really *need* to know the answer? What difference will the answer make to you? Will the truth help or harm you? Will you obsess over the answers you get, or will it bother you more to not ask the question? If you are both committed to saving your relationship, are the answers still important?

2. Create a safe space to get honest answers

Your partner needs to feel secure enough to open up to you with the answers to your questions. This requires you to stay calm so they can tell you things they may be afraid of revealing.

Remember, your partner is only human. They made a mistake, but they're trying to put it right. Try to stay in control of your emotional reactions and take a break if it all becomes too much. You're likely to hear some things that may make you want to retaliate. You need to stay on top of those urges. Behaving erratically, bad-mouthing your spouse to friends and family or contacting the other woman/man will only cause more damage to your relationship.

You might learn things that make you question whether the damage to your relationship can ever be repaired. Consider that your spouse will be feeling the same way. Make a promise to yourself and your partner that you will do your best to work through whatever comes up. It might feel like you won't survive this process in the heat of the moment, but I've seen couples come through seemingly impossible situations and be closer than ever.

3. Ask your questions

Once you've finalized your list of have-to-know questions, it's time for you to ask them. Your spouse needs to be ready to give honest answers, no matter how hard it might be. They should be committed to acting with compassion toward you, giving you the reassurance you need to stay together and rebuild trust. Supporting each other through this process is a powerful way to bring you closer together and start you on the road to healing.

Always remember that the goal is to understand what happened, not gain ammunition to use against the other. For this to work, you need to accept that at some point you'll need to put this in the past, even if you're not ready to do so right now. Working together as a team, you can fix what was broken.

Writing a Full Disclosure

We've discussed the importance of a written full disclosure. It's time for you to put pen to paper and write a first draft. The following questions will help you get your thoughts out. Not all of the questions will be relevant to your circumstances, so use the ones you need and ignore the rest. You might like to go over your disclosure with a therapist before sharing it with your spouse. You could also write the answers to each question on separate pieces of paper to leave space for follow-up questions from your therapist, accountability partner, or spouse.

- **Objectification.** When did you first notice yourself ranking people by their physical appearance? Did you feel an attraction toward certain qualities or strengths? How did you start rearranging your life to encounter, find favor with, or avoid people you found attractive? How did these adjustments make you feel isolated or fake? How did it lead you to start keeping secrets or telling lies?
- **Physical lust.** What are the most attractive features in the opposite sex? What locations or activities did you engage in to put yourself in the way of temptation? How did you organize your time so you could be around attractive people?
- **Lustful thoughts.** What romantic or erotic themes do you find yourself thinking about the most? What desires or insecurities do these address? What films or books encapsulate these themes? How much time do you spend watching or reading these? How much time do you spend fantasizing about these themes?
- **Soft porn.** What was your first experience with soft porn? What is your current experience with it? Do you sexualize any aspects of your current life, so they mimic soft porn? Do you have any rituals to prepare yourself for soft porn? What triggers a desire to indulge in soft porn? Do you use sexual activity as a reward for yourself?
- **Hard porn.** What was your first exposure to hard porn? How much time do you spend looking at porn

every week? How much money have you spent on it? Do you have any current subscriptions? Do you have pornography hidden anywhere, either physically or electronically? Do you have any secret email accounts?

- **Anonymous interactions.** Do you use any websites, phone lines, or other services to connect with other people for the purposes of sexual activity? Do you use any chat rooms, social networking sites or matchmaking services? How much time do you spend looking for someone to interact with? Are your real name and contact details listed anywhere? Have you sent photos of yourself (sexual or otherwise) or communicated over webcam? As you get to know someone via any of these methods, do you feel yourself becoming more attracted or less interested? Have you ever scheduled a meeting with anyone?
- **Emotional affairs.** How did the relationship begin, and when did the conversations cross the line? What negative statements have you made about your spouse or marriage? Have you told each other you're attracted? Do you have any means of hidden communication? When, where, and how do you talk? How have you hidden this from your spouse? How easy is it to hide the relationship? Do you go on dates? Was your behavior driven by a feeling of

unhappiness in your existing relationship or attraction to this new person?

- **Sexual touch without sex.** Did you hold hands, massage each other, hug, kiss, remove your clothing, fondle each other or engage in oral sex? How many people have you done this with? With each person, how many times? With each person over how long? What stopped you from taking the next step?
- **One-off sexual encounter.** How many people have you had one-off encounters with? Who pursued whom? Did you deliberately put yourself in temptation's way? Is there a possibility of pregnancy from any of these encounters? Have you paid for sex? Were alcohol or drugs involved?
- **Affairs.** In addition to answering the questions around emotional affairs, write about when the sex began. What percentage of your interactions with the other person was sexual? Did you make any expressions of love or commitment? (Verbal, gifts, trips, etc.) Was it a romantic relationship or more like friends with benefits? Who else knew about the relationship?
- **Longer-term affairs.** What plans did you make to leave your spouse? Did you do any research or put together any action steps? Did you introduce any family, friends, or children to your other partner? Did you protect your other partner emotionally or financially at the expense of your first spouse and

family? What lies did you tell yourself or others to justify your decisions?

Full Disclosure Follow-Up for the Betrayed Partner

After you've heard your spouse's full disclosure, take some time to reflect on what you've learned. You'll have more question and likely want to clarify certain details. Asking these whenever they pop into your mind will make it harder for you to assimilate everything you're told, and it can undermine the fragile trust you're trying to rebuild. What's more, random questions get random answers which can lead to paranoia, even if your spouse is being honest.

Keep a notebook handy and write down questions whenever they come up. Do this for a few days and then organize them. This will help you see your spouse's answers as part of a cohesive whole, making it easier for you to understand what they're saying.

You can organize your questions in a number of ways:

- Based on the full disclosure outline.
- Based on the history of your marriage/timeline of the affair.
- Based on the various themes.
- Based on the emotions behind each question.

As much as you desperately may want to know why, this is the one question I would advise against asking because there are no good answers. Either the answer sounds like your spouse is blaming you for not fulfilling their needs, or they genuinely have no idea, which will make you feel angry. Instead, seek to ask questions that will help you come to terms with what's happened.

If you feel that your spouse isn't being honest, tell them how you're feeling. Ask them what they can do to be more transparent so you can start to trust them again.

I advise against playing detective without your spouse's consent—this will only undermine the trust you're trying to build. Do not do anything illegal when trying to get to the heart of the matter, and don't let your desperation to uncover the truth become an obsession. Work with a therapist so you can put any fears or concerns into the right context.

In this chapter, we've looked deeply at the issue of honesty. You've learned about:

- Why people lie after an affair.
- The importance of being honest and how you can be fully open about what you've done.
- The obsession and depression cycles.
- The dos and don'ts about discussing your affair.
- Full disclosure and how you can put together your own document.

I cannot stress enough how essential honesty is to recover from an affair. If you don't feel you're going to be able to be honest, you should ask yourself some serious questions about the future of your relationship. Why are you afraid of being honest? You can't do any more damage than you already have. Being dishonest is what got you here in the first place. It's time to try a different way.

In the next chapter, we're going to explore a common emotion related to affairs: grief.

3

GRIEF

I diplomatically placed the box of tissues closer to the sobbing woman sitting opposite me.

"It's just so hard, you know? We've been together for over thirty years. I've always loved my husband. We've had three children together. Sure, we've had tough times, but I've always been there to support him. When he lost his job, I was there for him, letting him know I wasn't with him for his money. I loved him like I've never loved anyone else. And now I've found out that he's been having an affair for the past five years with a woman much younger than him. What am I supposed to do with that? Thirty years of marriage gone because he couldn't keep it in his pants. I feel like I don't know who he is. I don't know who *I* am. It's like my whole life is a lie, and I don't know what to do. I've lost everything. It's like my husband's died, only he's still here, still hurting me."

She broke down again, and all I could do was sympathize. When you find out your spouse has been cheating on you, grief is one of the most common reactions. You'll need to fully grieve the loss of the relationship you thought you had before you can move on. Grief is a difficult emotion and one which few of us fully understand. It's different for everyone. How you feel is how you feel.

HOW LONG WILL IT TAKE FOR ME TO RECOVER FROM MY SPOUSE'S AFFAIR?

While every circumstance is different, this is a rough timeline for the recovery process:

Zero to Six Weeks

This is the immediate aftermath of finding out about the affair when establishing what happened. You'll be feeling shocked, with emotions flying all over the place. Ideally, by the end of six weeks, the full story has come out, so you can move on to the next stage. If not, it'll be harder for you to rebuild trust.

Six Months

This is where you have to go through various actions so you can both feel secure in moving forward in your relationship. You need to feel your partner still cares and will be grieving the loss of the relationship you thought you had. They need to be doing whatever is necessary to give you the reassurance it won't happen again. You'll both need to explore the story behind why it happened.

Nine to Twelve Months

This is when you'll find yourself feeling ready to forgive, which will enable you to truly reconcile. You both should have a clear picture of why the affair happened, and your partner should have been working on themselves and reassuring you that they're genuinely committed to your marriage.

Twelve to Eighteen Months

Now you'll be ready to decide to move on together. Your relationship will have changed, but hopefully for the better. You'll have learned how you handle adversity together and developed better ways of communicating.

If the thought of your current situation going on for eighteen months is a source of stress, please try not to worry about it. If you're both putting in the time and energy, you'll see improvements much sooner than that. It's just that, in my experience, this is roughly the amount of time it takes to fully process your feelings about the affair.

FORGIVENESS

I often hear clients say, "If they would just forgive me, we could get past this." They seem to think that forgiveness is a magic wand they can wave to make everything right. As I'm sure you're aware, it doesn't really work like that.

I want to make it very clear what forgiveness is *not*:

- **Forgiveness is not ignoring your emotions.** Just because you forgive someone doesn't mean you aren't still hurting.
- **Forgiveness doesn't mean everything's okay.** It doesn't let your partner justify what they did or get away without any consequences.
- **Forgiveness doesn't excuse things.** It doesn't absolve your partner of responsibility for what they did.
- **Forgiveness is not forgetting.** You can't wipe the slate clean just by saying you're sorry.
- **Forgiveness doesn't restore trust.** It's the first step toward trusting, but it's not the whole story.
- **Forgiveness doesn't equate reconciliation.** You can forgive someone and still never want to deal with them again.

Put simply, forgiveness is releasing yourself from the affair's hold over you. It's choosing to let yourself move on rather than obsessing over what happened and allowing it to shape your future behavior. It is something you can do without the person who's wronged you ever doing anything. As much as it's nice when someone says sorry or tries to make amends, sometimes that's just not possible. You still have the power to forgive them.

There are three steps to forgiveness:

1. Acknowledging the harm, in this case, that an affair has occurred.
2. Admitting that amends need to be made, that something needs to be done to make up for that harm.
3. Releasing the other party from the need to make amends.

It's perfectly natural to want your partner to do something to make things right. We've already discussed some of those options. But when you forgive them, you choose not to let what they do have any power over you. Regardless of whether you decide to stay together or not, you allow yourself to move on to a brighter future.

If you feel that you can't forgive your spouse, that's okay. It's normal to take a while to be able to let go of past hurts. You should be aware that when you don't forgive someone, it can impact your physical, emotional, and spiritual health. In fact, when you forgive someone, it has nothing to do with making things easier for *them* and everything to do with making things better for *you*.

You can forgive someone and still put in place boundaries and strategies to ensure they won't repeat the behavior in the future. Fool me once, shame on you; fool me twice, shame on me.

But if you're serious about rebuilding your relationship, you're going to need to learn to trust again. And that can only come after you've forgiven them.

GRIEF

Recovering from betrayal is a process akin to grieving after a bereavement. You've lost the spouse you thought you had. You've lost the marriage you thought you had. You've lost your self-image of someone who knew their partner inside and out. So many losses—of course, you're going to need to grieve.

Grief is a highly misunderstood emotion. It's a deep anguish that strikes us to our very core and expresses itself in different ways. When someone you love betrays you, it feels like the ultimate personal attack. What's more, you don't get the same level of support you would have if your partner had died. There's no formal ritual to support you in saying goodbye to the past. Nobody rallies around to care for you. Instead, you're meant to just get over it or get out—there's no gray area.

Grief is an internal process as opposed to mourning, which is the external expression of grief. Grief can make one feel numb, sad, angry, regretful or even relieved, while mourning might involve talking, crying, or lashing out. Mourning enables you to process your grief, which is why it's so important to allow yourself to mourn in the way which is healthiest and most helpful for you.

Recognize that you've been hurt very badly. The pain runs deep. It's not something you'll just get over in a few weeks or even months. If you're finding yourself still struggling to move on and it's been a long time, say, ten months, ask yourself, *if my spouse had died, would I still be struggling?* Chances are, you'd answer yes.

You've been through a similar bereavement with losing the person you thought you knew. Allow yourself time and be kind to yourself.

Self-care following a betrayal

The most important thing when recovering from an affair is to be kind to yourself.

- **Express your grief.** Your emotions will be unpredictable and intense during this period. This is normal. Giving yourself permission to truly feel and work with your emotions rather than bottling them up will help you process them that much faster.

- **Don't blame yourself.** It's easy to blame yourself for what happened, especially if you suffer from low self-esteem. You can start telling yourself you're the one responsible for the infidelity because you weren't able to meet your spouse's needs in whatever way. Alternatively, you might be angry with yourself for not knowing something was wrong sooner. Beating yourself up over what happened won't help you heal. If you find yourself having these kinds of thoughts, come up with opposite statements to limit the damage. E.g., if you find yourself thinking, *I should have spent more time with him,* counter it with *I spent as much time as I could have. He could have made more time for me. His affair is not my fault.*
- **Look after yourself.** Infidelity can lead to hypervigilance and fear that your partner will cheat again if you don't do absolutely everything they want. Neglecting your needs to make someone else happy isn't sustainable and won't save your marriage.
- **Don't make any major decisions.** When we make decisions during times of emotional turmoil, we rarely make good choices. Don't make any knee-jerk reactions. You might decide you can't stay with your spouse, but don't make that decision immediately (unless your spouse is abusive). Give it some time before you decide to do something you might later regret.

- **Don't isolate yourself.** You may feel shame or humiliation that your spouse has cheated on you, stopping you from reaching out to someone for support. You may also find that you don't always get the support you need. If you go to a friend, for example, they may urge you to leave your spouse when you want to work on your marriage, which is why it's best to find someone who can be objective—such as a therapist. You might like to look into support groups, either in person or online. While these aren't right for everyone, many people find it useful to share their thoughts and experiences with people who are going through what they're going through. You even make new friends.

How to grieve

The way we grieve is shaped by many factors, such as how your family dealt with emotion, your experience of loss, your personality and gender, your culture, and whether you have a tendency to be a thinker, feeler, or doer. Grieving doesn't follow a rigid format and doesn't always have a step-by-step pattern.

You may have heard of the Kübler-Ross five stages of grief: denial, anger, bargaining, depression, and acceptance. You may even recognize them in yourself. I prefer to use J. William Worden's model of dealing with grief in tasks because it enables my clients to be more proactive when it comes to working through their grief.

The first task

Accept that you have suffered a loss. Common emotions are shock, numbness, and disbelief. Initially, this can make you appear strong when actually you're detached from your emotions. When your emotions come flooding back after the numbness wears off, it can be overwhelming.

The second task

Once you've accepted the loss of your previous marriage, it's time to work through the pain of grief. This task can involve you experiencing a broad range of emotions, including sadness, anxiety, anger, isolation, loneliness, guilt, and relief. You may even feel like you're going crazy because your emotions are so unstable. Be patient with yourself, and don't be afraid to get professional support as you go through this.

How to relate to your partner after an affair

You may decide it might be a good idea to temporarily separate after an affair. This will give you both time to process and adjust. Ask yourself whether you can stay under the same roof without verbally or even physically attacking each other. Question whether you can cope with seeing your spouse every day in your current emotional state. This will tell you whether you should take some time apart.

There are two different options if you decide to briefly separate. Separating and sleeping in different areas of the home and avoiding each other as much as possible may be the best option if you want to give yourselves the chance to work on your issues, minimize the impact on your children and limit the financial impact of a separation. One of you temporarily moving out might be a better choice if you cannot guarantee each other's emotional or physical safety, if the betrayed spouse can't bear to be around the other and if the cheater isn't ready to make amends or get help.

In the initial aftermath of an affair, couples frequently alternate between having long, intense fights, and acting as if nothing has happened, refusing to talk about the affair. Neither approach is particularly productive, which is why seeking help from a qualified therapist is a good idea to start a healthy dialog.

Some couples are unsure whether they should be having sex. Ultimately, this is down to the individual couple. Realistically, it comes down to whether being intimate would be helpful or unhelpful. The final decision should always lie with the betrayed spouse. At some point, you'll need to resume sexual relations, but when that time comes will depend on you.

It's normal not to want to have any sexual contact. It's also normal to experience a heightened sex drive as a means to reconnect with your spouse. Be aware that these feelings can change at any time and again; this is perfectly normal. Listen to yourself and respect how you feel.

I'd strongly advise you to get yourself tested for the full spectrum of sexually transmitted diseases, even if your partner says it's unnecessary. STDs are common and do not need full intercourse for someone to be infected. Be safe and make sure you're both uninfected.

Relearning how to communicate with your partner

I've said it before, and I'm going to repeat it before this book is done: communication is key to recovering from a betrayal. The one thing the cheater and the cheated on usually have in common is that they don't feel heard. Emotions cloud your thinking, and you get so caught up in your own pain that you struggle to listen to anyone else's. It doesn't take much for things to start off calmly only to rapidly descend into yelling, fighting, screaming, and tears. If you don't know how to talk to each other without getting lost like this, your problems can't ever be resolved, and you'll never rebuild your relationship. This is why getting support from a therapist is such a good idea—they can teach you new ways of communicating, such as:

- **Imago dialog.** This is a three-step process developed by Harville Hendrix, Ph.D. and Helen LaKelly Hunt, Ph.D. The steps are mirroring, validation, and empathy. It means you take the time to understand what your partner is telling you before considering your own response. It teaches you to appreciate your partner's experience without having to compromise your own.

- **Emotion-focused therapy.** This approach teaches you how to understand what your partner's emotions are telling you. So, for example, if something happens to remind your spouse of your betrayal, instead of getting annoyed with them for being upset, you can acknowledge that they're feeling hurt right now and encourage them to share what they're going through with you. By validating your partner's feelings, you show you care and are happy to help them heal. It can be difficult to do this when you feel your partner's emotional response is an attack, but it really can bring you together.
- **Monologs.** Sometimes it's hard for a couple to engage in a normal back-and-forth conversation. With the monolog approach, you agree on a set amount of time for one person to talk while the other person listens and takes notes. You then take a break, possibly even leaving it to the next day to return to the subject. This enables you to feel heard without being interrupted.
- **Keeping a diary.** Writing things out is a good way of exploring your feelings about the affair. It's a form of private communication which allows you to look at the situation with a certain amount of emotional distance. Writing lets you slow down and reflect on

what's happening so you can learn more about who you are and what you want. Keep your diary in a private and safe place so you know you can write without fear of your words causing any damage should someone else read them.

- **Write a letter.** This may be in the form of a disclosure letter, which we've discussed in the last chapter. A letter enables you to take the time to carefully consider the words you choose and how you want to communicate. Some people find that the simple act of writing a letter is all they need, and they don't send it to the intended recipient.

Emotional triggers during the grieving process

Emotional triggers are intrusive emotions and thoughts surrounding the affair. Your nervous system goes into overdrive, reacting to the situation as a threat. You experience a surge of adrenaline as your body prepares to deal with the threat. Once this has occurred, then the prefrontal cortex (the part of the brain controlling reasoning and higher-level thought) will analyze whether you're actually in danger.

Triggers are not:

- A means of punishing the cheater.
- A sign of unforgiveness.
- A profound insight into your spouse or the situation. (We may feel the thoughts we have when we're in this heightened state are clear when, in fact, they are heavily influenced by our emotions.)
- A setback.

In reality, triggers are an opportunity to do some more healing and reconnect with your partner.

If you are the one who cheated:

- **Approach your spouse with compassion and gentle curiosity.** It is your job now to understand and support your spouse. This involves accepting your own shame and guilt over the situation.
- **Do not avoid your spouse's pain.** It's hard to deal with someone else's pain, especially when you're the one who caused it. But this will make your spouse feel even more abandoned and alone. Be willing to be there for them when they're dealing with a trigger or give them space if that's what they need.
- **See the hurt and fear behind the anger.** Your spouse's anger is coming from a place of pain. When you can remember that, it makes it easier to stay calm.

Conversation starters could involve things like:

- Help me understand how I hurt you.
- I'm not going anywhere. I'm here for you.
- I'm going to work with you to understand why this happened.
- I'll answer any questions, even if you've already asked them.
- It's okay to talk about [the trigger] as much as you need.
- What are you feeling right now?

If you're the one who was cheated on:

- **Understand that triggers are an opportunity for you to process your pain.** You don't want to feel the way you do, but it is what it is. Processing your pain allows you to move through it rather than burying it, so it continues to haunt you.
- **Talk about the trigger.** This will help you process what's going on so you can heal.
- **Make sure you get compassion and care from your spouse.** It's important that you feel they care about what you're going through and support you while you're struggling.
- **Put plans in place so you can actively see your spouse working to figure out why they did what**

they did. They need to demonstrate they're willing to own up to what they did, accept the consequences and learn more about themselves.

I give my clients a five-step process to work through triggers:

1. Acknowledge what's happened

If you're the betrayed spouse, pay attention when you're being triggered, when you recognize the onset of a triggered response. Be kind to yourself. Let yourself experience the emotions rather than trying to bury them.

If you're the cheater, don't tell your spouse that they're being triggered. Instead, support them through their feelings and don't tell them to stop feeling the way they do. Tell them you're here for them and willing to listen to anything they need to say.

2. Identify the trigger

If you're the betrayed spouse, consider whether you're responding to a current threat, such as your spouse being secretive, trying to make you feel guilty or becoming defensive, or whether you're reacting to a memory. This will help you make sense of what's happening and what you need to do to further process the affair.

If you're the cheater, consider how you're feeling in this moment. If you're getting angry, it's likely that this is masking underlying guilt and shame. Notice if you find yourself getting defensive, aggressive or manipulative to avoid dealing with your shame and guilt and work to be more supportive of your spouse.

3. Ask for what you need

If you're the betrayed spouse, think about what would be most helpful for you right now. Do you need to talk to someone, be by yourself, or spend time with your spouse or a friend? Don't be afraid to say what you need and then give it to yourself.

If you're the cheater, listen to what your spouse needs and do your best to give it to them, even if it means answering the same questions again. Appreciate that your spouse isn't being intentionally provocative or unforgiving. They are simply going through the healing process.

4. What to do when you talk

If you're the betrayed spouse, don't use threats to get your point across, such as saying you'll leave or have an affair of your own. If you follow through, it'll only cause more damage. Telling your spouse, "You've really hurt me," is more powerful than "I need to sleep with someone else, so you know how this feels."

If you're the cheater, keep your focus on your spouse's feelings rather than yours. Don't say things like: "I'm sorry" or "I wish I'd done things differently." This keeps the spotlight on you. Instead, reflect back to your spouse what they're telling you. This lets them know you care about their feelings.

5. Be grateful for the triggers

While they're unpleasant, triggers are an opportunity to take a long look at ourselves and our relationship without rose-colored glasses to see what's really going on. They bring up a lot of trash, but this is a chance to clear it out once and for all.

When you ask, "What do I need to do?" you can move forward together on your healing journey.

Who to talk to about the affair

It's a good idea to be discerning whom you discuss the affair with. Before deciding whom to talk to about the affair, think carefully about whether someone is safe or unsafe.

Safe people:

- Give you unconditional love and acceptance.
- Can sit with your grief rather than telling you to move on or try to distract you from it.
- Don't gossip.
- Don't try to fix things or give solutions.

- Can handle angry outbursts and strong emotions.
- Understand that we're all human and flawed.
- Offer love rather than advice.

Unsafe people:

- Play the blame game.
- Deny what's happened or minimize it.
- Try to fix the situation.
- Give unwanted advice.
- Gossip.
- Are only there for you if you're happy and aren't going through a tough time.
- Are arrogant or self-righteous.

Once you've identified good people to talk to, ask them to go to lunch or have a coffee with you. Tell them you've got things going on and you'd like to talk about it with them. Tell them what you need from them. So if you're looking for a sounding board, tell them that. Likewise, let them know if you do or don't want their advice and let them know if you're working with a therapist, so they don't have to take on that role.

Not everyone needs to know what's happened but having a few supportive people around you who are aware of the details can be really helpful and just what you need to make it through.

If children are involved, they need to know what's happened, but you should present the information in a careful, age-appropriate manner. Just as you've taken the time to consider whether you're going to stay or go, you should also take your time in deciding when and how to talk to your children.

Don't make promises you may not be able to keep. You might promise that you're not splitting up, but if your partner continues with their affair, you may decide to end your marriage. If that happens, your children will be upset with you for breaking your promise.

Tell your children that you're going through a rough time and trying to figure things out, but you both love them very much. "I don't know" is a perfectly acceptable answer and is less damaging than telling them something which turns out to be wrong further down the line.

You might like to discuss with your therapist what to tell your children. And above all, never say anything derogatory to your children about your spouse.

Exercises

Couples counseling exercise for infidelity

Answer the following questions with your spouse:

1. What are the triggers connected to the affair?
2. How do you feel when you're triggered?

As you share your thoughts about your triggers with your partner, be as open and honest as possible to build closer connections. If you're the one listening to the answers, don't judge or criticize. Simply ask your spouse what you can do to support them.

Being able to identify and work through triggers will help bring the two of you together. After an affair, it's natural to put up defensive walls which get in the way of building bridges. Being open and honest about your triggers will help bring down these walls.

Put yourself in your partner's shoes

If you're the cheater, sit down and make a list of forty different things which might trigger your partner. This isn't aimed at shaming or condemning your partner for overreacting—quite the opposite. Instead, this is a way for you to try and appreciate what they're currently going through and how you can be more aware of their triggers and needs. You can then talk about this together and see what you can both do to make your spouse feel safer and more secure.

In this chapter, we examined grief. You learned about:

- The timeline of grief.
- The power of forgiveness.
- Practicing self-care following infidelity.
- How to grieve effectively.

- Relearning how to communicate.
- Triggers and how to deal with them.

In the next chapter, we're going to look at what you can do to make amends and start to move past what's happened.

4

MAKING AMENDS

I looked at the couple sitting on the couch opposite me. "What made you book a session with me?" I asked.

They glanced at each other, each seeming to encourage the other to be the first to speak. At last, the woman, Liz, said, "I had an affair."

I smiled to reassure her. "You're not the first person to tell me that, and I'm sure you won't be the last. What do you hope to achieve by coming to see me?"

"We want to save our marriage," her husband, Mike, told me. "I mean, I really want to save our marriage. I'm just not sure if it's possible."

"I'm not going to make any promises," I said. "But if you both want to make it work, we can certainly do our best to figure out what went wrong and see if we can put it right."

Over the course of our time together, we managed to get to the heart of what happened. Liz had lost her father at an early age, which left her with feelings of abandonment. She never felt good enough, did everything she thought Mike wanted at the expense of her own happiness and avoided conflict at all costs because she felt that if she fought with Mike, he'd leave her. Over time, she lost sight of who she was, and because she'd been so focused on pleasing Mike, she'd neglected her own needs.

Liz met a man at work who started flirting with her. She felt like she could be herself with him because she had nothing to lose. This feeling of freedom and acceptance she experienced with her co-worker eventually led to her having a physical affair.

It took a lot of work for Liz to understand how her childhood experiences had brought her to this place. At the same time, Mike needed a great deal of support to understand how Liz could love him and cheat on him. It took a while, but eventually, he was able to see that it was because she loved him. She was afraid of losing him by being herself, which was part of the reason why she turned to someone else.

Both of them did a lot of work on themselves to overcome their issues. Mike worked to find the compassion for Liz's feelings while healing his own.

A lot of this was only possible because Liz took full responsibility for her choices. She worked hard to make amends and rebuild trust with her husband. She started to open up to Mike about her thoughts and feelings, while Mike listened and didn't take advantage of her vulnerabilities.

Together, they took the shattered pieces of their marriage and reconnected with each other through sharing their innermost thoughts, listening to each other and consciously choosing to be compassionate and kind. While they both would have preferred for the affair not to have happened, by the time they stopped coming to me, they had created a marriage that was stronger and closer than anything they'd ever experienced previously.

Making amends is not optional

When someone has been hurt, they're more likely to forgive the person who hurt them if that person actively takes steps to make amends. Making amends is key to repairing a relationship after you've broken someone's trust or hurt them. Even if your partner minimizes your attempts or isn't ready to accept your apology, it's important you do your best to right the wrong. This acknowledges what you've done and helps pave the way to fixing things.

When you make amends, you're accepting responsibility for your transgressions. The more you can do this without blaming the other person or making excuses, the more sincere your efforts to rebuild the relationship will appear.

Be consistent

Making amends isn't a shortcut to getting back to the way things were (which is impossible). It's simply the best way to get back on track to building a new, more positive relationship. This is a long-term approach because proving you are willing to do things differently requires diligent, daily action that demonstrates you are making a change. You are choosing to be honest, respectful and humble, and you can only show this by behaving in a way that is consistent and authentic.

When you decide to make amends, you will need to assume it will take time for your partner to recover from your affair. You may be feeling guilty, shameful, or humiliated, so don't want to discuss the affair or shut down the conversation when it does come up. You need to allow your partner to talk about things as they need in an open, empathic manner. Showing you can accept the blame and deal with your feelings of guilt or remorse without reflecting this back at your partner or walking away from the conversation will do a lot to prove you are worthy of trust.

You will need to respect any new restrictions or rules your partner wants to put in place. After all, they've got good reason to be mistrustful of you, so if they want to see your emails, phone logs, etc., accept that this is how it is—at least right now. You've got nothing to hide anymore . . . have you?

Be open to making any changes necessary to put your relationship in a better place. Accept that this may even mean big life changes, such as changing jobs or moving out of the area to get away from your ex-lover. If you're dedicated to saving your relationship, you'll need to do what it takes. There are always other jobs and other homes. You'll never have another marriage like the one you have.

MAKING AMENDS VS. APOLOGIZING

We say "I'm sorry" so many times that the words often lose their meaning. It seems like an easy 'get out of jail free' card to toss out when you've done something wrong, and magically everything's okay.

When it comes to infidelity, saying "I'm sorry" are never going to be enough to undo the damage caused by your cheating. Not only that, but it may also sound insulting like you're dismissing the enormity of what happened.

Making amends takes things to the next level. It is the process of understanding the extent of what you've done and finding a different way. It is a lifestyle choice rather than a one-off gesture. It is something that requires repeated action, discipline, and a focus on the long-term future of your relationship. Moreover, it puts the focus on your partner rather than yourself. You are reaching out to them to show you still care and want to put their needs as your highest priority.

HOW DO I KNOW MY PARTNER IS READY TO MAKE AMENDS?

As we've already discussed, words aren't enough when it comes to rebuilding your relationship. If you're the person who's been betrayed, you'll be so used to hearing lies that it's no wonder you're struggling with believing your partner when they say they want to put things right.

There are a few things that will tell you your partner is ready to make amends:

- **They are empathic toward you.** They make an active attempt to listen to your needs and meet them with their actions.
- **They can disagree with you in healthy and productive ways.** It's natural for you to have arguments on the road to recovery. It's how you deal with these disagreements that shows you whether your partner is truly willing to make amends. If your partner is able to take your view on board without casting aspersions on you, this is a good sign that they're ready to do things differently.
- **They use their actions to show they care.** Talk is cheap. Now is the time for your partner to show you

how much they want to rebuild things. If you see a concerted effort and willingness to do things differently, take hope from it.

- **They understand the need to earn your trust.** It's going to take time, and they accept that and give you what you need to start trusting again—no matter how long it takes.

I've been unfaithful – how can I make amends?

There are many benefits to making amends:

- It gives you emotional relief in a way nothing else can. It allows you to know you've done everything you can to repair the damage, regardless of the outcome.
- It helps you feel good about yourself. It takes a lot of courage to admit to what you've done and be willing to do something about it. You should recognize that this is a big deal and give yourself credit for that.
- It can help restore trust. Actively demonstrating you're working on your relationship gives your partner a clear sign that you're worth trusting again.
- It allows you to resolve unfinished situations. You've put an end to your affair, and now you're ready to move forward with your partner.
- It reduces worry and stress. Everything's out in the open, and you don't need to fear your partner finding out your secrets because they know them all.

Still, it can be difficult to know where to start. One approach I like to use with my clients is the H.U.R.T. technique:

- **H – Hurt**

Tell your partner what you did to hurt them. Don't get into the reasons why or what your motives were. Simply share the facts of the situation.

- **U – Understanding**

Tell your partner how you think your behavior made them feel and acknowledge and validate them.

- **R – Remorse**

Express remorse for what you did and tell your partner how it makes you feel about yourself. This goes deeper than saying sorry—dive into *why* you're sorry and what exactly you regret about your actions.

- **T – Time**

Let your partner know it's going to take time to heal your relationship, and you're willing to give it as long as it takes. By the same token, it's going to take time to deal with your own issues so you don't stray again, and you'd like your partner to allow you that time so you can both build a future together.

EMOTIONAL RESTITUTION (FOR THE ONE WHO WAS UNFAITHFUL)

Earlier in this book, we looked at Full Disclosure, in which the partner who cheated took ownership of what happened with a focus on their betrayal. Accepting responsibility for what you've done was just the first step in making amends. Now you're going to build on that with emotional restitution, which puts the spotlight on how your infidelity has hurt those around you, especially your spouse.

Start by making an emotional restitution statement. This encapsulates what you're willing to do on an ongoing basis to make amends and heal your relationship.

Your statement might look something like this:

I am committed to moving forward with my husband/wife, acknowledging that we have both been hurt by my actions. I accept the consequences of my infidelity and will work on processing my grief over what happened while supporting my husband/wife to work through theirs. I am willing to explore the details of my infidelity and the surrounding emotions with my husband/wife. I am dedicated to working together with my husband/wife to overcome the various problems my infidelity has caused us.

Let's break this down a little further:

I am committed to moving forward with my husband/wife, acknowledging that we have both been hurt by my actions.

While you were having an affair, you were being deceitful and abandoning your marriage. With this statement, you're deciding to live in the reality of your relationship, even if it's painful. And where the pair of you are feeling hurt and struggling, you're agreeing to face this pain head-on rather than trying to avoid it. You are working together on this rather than continuing to abandon your marriage.

I accept the consequences of my infidelity and will work on processing my grief over what happened while supporting my husband/wife to work through theirs.

Your actions have cost both of you dearly. You've lost the marriage you thought you had. As we've already discussed, you need to grieve this. While you can do this by yourself, when you choose to work through your grief together, you open yourself up to a healing process that can bring you both together, so neither of you has to feel alone.

I am willing to explore the details of my infidelity and the surrounding emotions with my husband/wife.

Difficult though it may be, you need to process what happened, so it doesn't happen again. This is going to be hard, and it's natural to want to avoid doing this, but if you're serious about being faithful from now on, it's an essential part of the healing journey. You need to be open to discussing your affair as much as necessary, which may be a lot when you first start working through it. Be open to exploring both you and your spouse's feelings and experiences. This is how you're going to process and assimilate it to move past it.

I am dedicated to working together with my husband/wife to overcome the various problems my infidelity has caused us.

Your affair has made life difficult for both of you. That's a fact you'll need to deal with. If you're able to work through it together, you'll both end up in a much better place down the line.

BLOCKS TO EMOTIONAL RESTITUTION

Making amends is challenging, and you may find yourself resisting the process. It can be useful to know about potential blocks to making emotional restitution so you can recognize them if they come up and put strategies in place to overcome them:

- **I've already acknowledged what I've done. I can't do any more than that.** Accepting responsibility is important, but it's not going to heal your marriage by itself. You need to do the hard work to show your spouse you've genuinely changed your behavior.

- **Obsessing over my infidelity causes more harm than good. We need to move on.** Yes, you need to move on, but that can't happen if you haven't both fully processed what happened. You may feel you've already dealt with your feelings, but your spouse may take a lot longer. You need to be willing to give them the time they need to come to terms with their new normal.
- **It's hurting my spouse more to dwell on my infidelity.** No, it hurts them more to brush it under the carpet and pretend it never happened. You need to face what happened and deal with the consequences head-on.
- **Dealing with my infidelity is too painful, so I don't want to do it.** It's tough to work through what you've done, but if you don't fully process what happened, you leave the door open to it happening again.
- **No one understands me.** You're not the only person to have been unfaithful, and sadly, you won't be the last. A good therapist will be able to support you unconditionally without judgment and give you the space to work through your experiences.
- **If I do the recovery work, everyone will just tell me I'm an awful person.** I can't promise you that hurtful things won't be said during this period, but if you're both genuine about healing your relationship, it's not about blaming or throwing insults around.

The focus is very much on solutions and what you can do together to move forward.

THE STEPS TO WRITING AN EMOTIONAL RESTITUTION LETTER

You may find yourself staring at a blank page when it comes to writing your emotional restitution letter. This format will give you a framework to build upon. The best thing you can do is just start writing. You can always go back and improve what you've written later, but you can't do that if you've got nothing to work with. Take your time. There's no hurry. It's better to get it right, and the effort you put into this sends a very clear signal to your spouse that you're serious about working things out.

1. I am solely responsible for my infidelity

This is a very important starting point for your letter. You chose to be unfaithful. It doesn't matter the circumstances. You could have made a different choice, but you didn't. Your spouse is likely to blame themselves at least partly for what happened, and you need to reassure them that they shouldn't. Your marriage may not have been perfect, but infidelity was not the way to fix it. List out how your partner was honoring your vows while you were breaking them to show them you're serious about accepting fault.

2. These are the ways in which I deceived you and others

When you cheat, you engage in deceit and manipulation in a bid to avoid being caught out. Now is the time to own up to all the ways in which you tried to cover up your affair, including directly lying, lying by omission, and building an image of yourself to cover your secret life.

Once you've listed these out, move on to examining the damage you think your lies caused, which allows you to build empathy for your partner.

3. I take full responsibility for the consequences of my actions

In Full Disclosure, you told your spouse what happened. Now you're going to face up to the damage your actions have caused. Actively listing out all those consequences will help you work through your grief with your spouse because you know exactly what you've lost. Areas you might like to consider include:

- Who you harmed.
- The emotional damage caused.
- Any physical damage.
- Financial implications.
- Harm to your sexual relationship.
- The damage done to your spouse's self-image.

- The impact on other people.

4. I am putting down my weapons

By 'weapons,' we mean the means we use to stop our spouse from discussing our infidelity, the defense mechanisms you put in place to protect yourself from exploring the impact of what you've done. List out the weapons you use and agree to stop those behaviors. These may be:

- **Hiding behind your shame.** Saying things like: "I'm a failure" or "I'll never be able to be good enough for you" are a way of facing what you've done and actually being emotionally present.
- **Going on the attack.** Accusing your partner of being unforgiving or being the one stopping you from healing adds to the pain of what you've done and sidesteps taking responsibility for your actions.
- **Making threats.** If you tell your spouse you're going to leave, take the children, ruin them financially, etc.., or even yell and throw things, you're shutting down the conversation and controlling how your partner is allowed to handle the situation.
- **Being emotionally distant.** Approaching things 'logically' means you're avoiding your emotions and those of your spouse, which means you can't fully engage in the healing process.

- **Minimizing your behavior.** What you did was wrong. Making your spouse question their reaction or perceptions means you're trying to avoid actively facing up to the damage you've done.
- **Rationalizing or justifying your behavior.** There are no excuses. Trying to convince yourself and/or your spouse that what you did was somehow acceptable only avoids dealing with the consequences.
- **Turning on the charm.** You may be a highly charismatic person. Heck, that may be what got you into this situation in the first place. But falling back on your charm is a way of avoiding digging deep into what brought you to this place. It's time to face up to who you really are.
- **Rewarding your spouse with affection and attention when they don't mention your infidelity.** You might be kidding yourself that it's a good day if you don't discuss your affair, but all you're doing is delaying facing up to your problems. It's a good day when you can both be authentic, connect to how you're really feeling and build bridges with each other.

5. I am willing to be accountable, so you can trust me

The loss of trust is a big deal. Your spouse is going to need you to be accountable so they can regain their trust in you. You need to show you understand why they need you to be open and accountable without trying to shame them or make them feel guilty. Write out some ideas of how you're willing to be accountable to them.

6. Share your pain

Your spouse needs you to be willing to explore the pain you've caused. They need to know they can feel anger, sadness, fear, or whatever else with you. Let them know that it's okay for them to express whatever emotions come up. Feeling this pain together will help you heal together.

7. Express gratitude

Close your letter by letting them know how much you appreciate them. Tell them how much it means to you that they're willing to work on your relationship with you. Finally, close with how much you're grateful for them as a person and that you accept them unconditionally. Don't ask for forgiveness in this letter. Simply close it with an expression of love.

Moving forward

Schedule time every thirty days to revisit the promises you've made in your emotional restitution letter. Evaluate how well you've been doing in living up to your commitments and look to where you can do better. Be accountable and if you've fallen short in any way, accept and acknowledge it with humility and think of ways you can change in the future.

IMPACT LETTER (FOR THE ONE WHO WAS BETRAYED)

Now that you know exactly what's happened, your impact letter is your chance to let your spouse know how their actions have affected you. This is going to be an emotional experience, so make sure to be kind to yourself during this process, taking as much time as you need to write your letter. You don't have to write it in one sitting. You can take a break as often as you need. There's no pressure and no deadline.

1. **Introduction**

Start the letter with why you are writing it and your hopes for how your partner will receive it.

2. Your experience

This section is where you write about the negative effect of your partner's behavior. Consider how it's impacted you cognitively, physically, emotionally, sexually, and experientially. Write as much as you need, no matter how long this section ends up being. You might like to start with a bullet list to jot down your ideas and then come back to expand on them.

3. How you've processed things

This is where you detail the various stages you've gone through following your discovery of the affair. Write out a timeline of the highs and lows, the various events and how they affected you. You may also like to include what was happening in your life before you found out about the affair and how the affair changed things.

4. What you need moving forward

This is where you detail what you're going to need from your spouse in the future. This might include therapy, regular check-ins, access to their phone, etc.

5. Your hopes for the future

Describe what you would like to see happening in the future for you, your partner, and your relationship.

6. Conclusion

End your letter by thanking your partner for listening and telling them what you'd like from them in response.

Example impact letter

Dear John,

I am writing this letter to let you know how your actions have affected me and what I've been going through ever since I learned about your affair. I hope you will read this letter with an open mind and heart, respecting where I am and listening without judgment or defensiveness. I am not writing this to hurt you, but you may hear things that are uncomfortable, and I would ask that you set aside any pain this may cause you so you can understand and appreciate my experience.

I am being vulnerable in this letter, which took a lot of courage to write. You have broken my trust through your actions. I cannot believe anything you say. I hate that when you tell me you love me, I question whether you're telling the truth, but right now, I have to question ***everything*** *you say.*

I would love to trust you again, but when I was sitting in the doctor's waiting room after being tested for STIs, I couldn't help thinking about how the only reason I was there was because of you. I can't stop obsessing over what you did. When I go out, I find myself wondering whether you've been to the same bar with her. The lies you told me were so convincing that it's got me wondering whether you are capable of being honest with me.

I do not feel secure in our relationship right now, and I feel so angry about it. I can't believe you could do this to our marriage. It feels like you've abandoned me and that also makes me feel sad and lonely. When we exchanged our vows, I never thought you'd make me feel this way.

As you know, I lost my job just before I found out about your affair, and I haven't been able to find another one because I've been so distracted by thoughts of you with her. This has impacted the family finances and undermines my self-esteem and self-worth because I feel like I'm not making the contribution to the household that I should be.

I find my body tensing when you try to hug me, and I can't relax around you. I've been trying to meditate so I can get my mental health back on an even keel. You used to make me feel like you were the one person who accepted me and loved me for who I am, but now there's a distance between us, and I don't know if we'll ever be able to get past it. Our conversations are difficult, and when we try to talk, we end up arguing because I'm so mad at you.

I'm afraid to tell you how I feel because I'm opening myself up to being hurt again, but I'm doing this because I really want us to work through this. I need you to commit to coming to therapy with me as well as therapy by yourself. I want to be able to check your phone at random times so I can reassure myself you're not in contact with her anymore. If you still care about me, I need you to show me, not just by telling me you love me, but by doing these things so we can try and rebuild our trust.

For all that you've hurt me, I still love you. I feel like you've lost yourself somewhere along the way, and I need you to find your way back to us. I want to feel like you're putting our marriage first, and I want to see you fighting for us.

Thank you for reading this. I would like you to take some time to think about what I've written, and then, when you're ready, write your response so we can continue to work through this without getting into another argument.

With love and hope,

Jane

EXERCISES

If you are the one who cheated, write an emotional restitution letter.

If you are the one who was betrayed, write an impact letter.

Share your letters with each other. You may prefer to do this in a therapeutic setting, so you have the support of an impartial observer.

As a bonus exercise, the one who strayed may like to write an impact letter from the perspective of your spouse. This will help you consider how your partner is feeling and enable you to actively listen to their own impact letter.

In this chapter, we looked at how you can start to make amends. You learned about:

- The importance of making amends.
- How making amends is different from apologizing
- How you can use the H.U.R.T. technique to start making amends.
- How to write an emotional restitution letter so you can start actively putting things right.
- How to write an impact letter so your partner can fully understand the effect of their actions.

In the next chapter, we're going to look at how you can take full accountability for your actions and develop empathy for your partner so you can rebuild your relationship on a stronger foundation.

5

TAKING FULL ACCOUNTABILITY AND DEVELOPING EMPATHY

"I'm really proud of you both," I said to the couple in my office. "You've done a lot of work to get to this stage, but there's still a long way to go."

"How much longer?" Julian, the one who had strayed, had always been impatient with the process, although, to his credit, he'd tried to hide his feelings and support his wife.

"It varies with every couple," I told him. "But there is a roadmap for you to follow. It's up to you how long it takes for you to get through each stage."

"What are the stages?" asked Anne, his wife.

"First of all, there's personal accountability," I said. "Julian needs to take full accountability for his actions." I looked at him directly. "That was your choice, so if you're trying to offset any of the blame for your affair on Anne, you're not being accountable, and it's going to be difficult for you to save your marriage."

"It's okay," Julian said. "I know this situation is completely my fault. I could have spoken to Anne about how I was feeling instead of turning to Beth." Anne winced at the sound of the name but said nothing. "I just wish Anne would get over it and realize I'm not going to do it again," Julian went on.

"That's the second step in this process," I said. "Patience. You've done all the right things, but Anne is going to need as long as it takes for her to recover. The more you pressure her to get over it, the less you're being truly accountable. You hurt her, and you need to deal with the consequences of that. If you can't, it would be better for you to leave."

"I'm not going to do that." Julian took his wife's hand.

"Good. But if you're serious about staying, you need to stop pressuring Anne to get over it so you can feel better."

"I'll try." Julian nodded.

"Next, you'll have to follow through. Anne will be watching closely to see if your actions match your words. If you say you're going to do something, do it, even if it seems trivial. If you say you're going to pick the kids up from school, be there. If you say you're going to arrange a date night, make it happen. These little things add up. They may seem like they're unrelated to your infidelity but, in fact, they're important evidence that you can be trusted again."

"I can do that," Julian promised.

"Be prepared to be vulnerable," I warned him. "It's very common among unfaithful people to struggle to be vulnerable with their spouse. An affair is an indication of other problems in your relationship. And many people find it easier to open up to their lover than to their wife because there's less on the line. You need to take emotional risks in letting Anne see the real you. Be transparent with your feelings, and she'll be more likely to trust you."

"I'll try." Julian looked a little overwhelmed by everything I was saying.

"It's not all down to you, though," I said. "Anne, you've also got to do your part. The pair of you need to agree on boundaries. Anne, you should feel free to express how you feel, but that doesn't mean you can descend into verbal abuse. If you're having a discussion and it starts to get heated, take time out. It's better to take a step back than to say something which causes even more harm. One of the reasons why Julian had an affair was because he felt he couldn't fully express himself, so we're all going to work on giving you both strategies for effective communication."

"I'll try," Anne said. "I just get so mad, you know?"

"I do know." I smiled at her. "And that's okay. It's all part of the process. But I want to warn you both right now that you need to both try to detach yourself from the outcome. You could do all the right things, and the other one could still decide they don't want to be in the marriage anymore. Or you might not be fully committed to the process, but your partner may feel they have to stay because they don't want to be alone. You can't control what your spouse does. You only have power over what you do. So set an intention right now that you're going to do your best and let go of any expectations. If your marriage is meant to last, it will."

That roadmap is one I give to all my clients. It's a long road to recovery following an affair, but many couples manage to make it through.

One good way of predicting whether a couple is likely to survive is whether they both take responsibility for their part in what happened.

TAKING RESPONSIBILITY

You both need to take responsibility for your role in what happened rather than falling into the trap of the blame cycle. This is where you point the finger at each other for the affair. One says, "You were lying and cheating. It's all your fault," while the other counters with, "You stopped talking to me, our sex life was nonexistent, and all you ever did was put me down. You shut me out!"

The simple reality is that an affair isn't an automatic reaction to a marriage in trouble. Many couples have problems but choose not to have an affair. Likewise, you can have a couple who love each other, yet one still has an affair.

You always have options. You could get therapy, turn to family, friends, or your church, or even separate or divorce rather than cheat.

It's best to avoid blaming at all. Often, unfaithful partners look to their spouse to share the blame, but this only compounds the hurt. Yes, you both made mistakes in your marriage, but if you ask your spouse to share the blame for your choices, you will make them wonder if you're going to have another affair the next time they make a mistake. Alternatively, the betrayed partner may accept the blame and try to earn their way back into their spouse's affections, meaning that the unfaithful person avoids tackling the underlying reasons why the affair happened—so the real problems are never dealt with.

If you cheated, accept responsibility for your decisions and understand there is never any justification for infidelity.

Here are some things you need to consider and discuss with your partner when taking responsibility for your actions:

- Look back at your relationship commitments and how you broke your vows.

- Examine how you allowed your boundaries to fall, so an affair was possible.
- Think about the opportunities you had to choose not to have an affair. Think about those moments where you could have made a different decision, leading to a different result.
- Acknowledge your partner's efforts when they sensed your marriage was in trouble, and be honest about how you failed to respond to those efforts.
- Did you minimize your behavior? Did you dismiss a romantic encounter as “just” a drink with a friend? Look at how you rationalized your behavior by minimizing what was going on.
- How did you rationalize your behavior? Explore how you fooled both your partner and yourself as you tried to justify what you were doing.
- Own up to any lies you told, either directly or by omission. Discuss how you deceived your partner and how you're going to do things differently from now on.
- Think about how you gaslighted your spouse by creating false narratives to explain what you were doing. Accept how damaging this was.

Try not to tell your spouse you still loved them while you were cheating. This undermines your efforts to acknowledge and validate the fact that you chose to stray. Instead, be prepared to repeat (many times!), "I chose to have an affair, which was the wrong decision." You cannot say this enough, and the more you repeat it, the more you convey to your partner the truth of the matter, absolving them of any self-blame.

HOW ACCOUNTABILITY WORKS

Many couples complain to me that they tell their spouse that something isn't working, or they ask them to do something different (like make as much time for them as they do for their friends), but they don't get a positive response. This is very common in long-term relationships. We fall into a rut, taking the other person for granted. So when they make a request like this, it sounds like they're complaining or criticizing instead of what they're really doing—working on your relationship.

This pattern of behavior is particularly common among couples who are dealing with infidelity.

You need to be accountable for your actions. This is how it works:

- Listen to what your partner is saying with an open mind. Try to be objective so you can minimize emotional reactivity.
- If you find yourself having an emotional response or wanting to overreact, take time out to think about

what you've heard so you can respond in a calmer manner.

- When you're ready to respond, start by agreeing with your partner. So, for example, if your partner asks you to stop leaving your wet towel on the floor, a good opening answer is, "You're right. I do leave my wet towel on the floor."
- Apologize if you were in the wrong in any way.
- Think about whether you can say yes to what your spouse is asking. If you can't immediately agree, tell them you need some time to think about it. That way, you won't make a knee-jerk reaction that could raise tensions or agree to something you have no intention of sticking to.
- If you agree to what your partner is saying, honor their request.

Believe it or not, your partner will respect and admire you more when you own up to and apologize for your mistakes. Try it. You'll soon see I'm right!

HOW DO I KNOW MY PARTNER WON'T CHEAT AGAIN?

There's a saying, 'once a cheater, always a cheater.' While this isn't always right, it is true that a significant proportion of people who stray will do it again regardless of the consequences. So how do you know your partner is going to stay faithful to you in the future? Here are a few red flags to watch out for:

- **They lie or keep secrets.** Even if the affair is over, your spouse may have fallen into the habit of lying, so they continue to deceive you. This can harm a relationship as much as cheating does—and can be a sign that they're prepared to betray you again.
- **They fail to be accountable for their behavior.** If they blame anyone except themselves for their affair, then they're not ready to accept responsibility and be accountable for what happened, which is essential to the healing process.
- **They apologize but expect you to be over it straight away.** We've already discussed that apologies aren't anywhere enough to repair the damage caused by an affair. If your partner thinks that it is, and you're not ready to move past it yet, they may decide they may as well have another affair.
- **They try to buy your forgiveness.** Gifts aren't going to undo the harm caused by an affair. If your partner starts trying to buy their way out of the situation, it could be a sign that another affair is brewing.
- **They use aggression or threaten you.** If this is the case, you may be better off ending the relationship. The cheater may threaten divorce or say they'll remove financial support, bullying their partner into submission. It's impossible to heal a relationship in

these circumstances, and it's not a healthy way of being.
- **They tell you to calm down.** If they tell you you're overreacting, they're not willing to accept the pain they've caused and would prefer you to make them feel better by denying your feelings.

If your partner is behaving in this way, it can be just as painful as an affair. None of them mean that your relationship is automatically over or that you can't fix it, but it's a clear sign that there's a lot of work to be done.

TRAUMA BONDING

We've already discussed in previous chapters how an affair can cause real trauma. I'd like to take a moment to discuss one potential impact of this—trauma bonding. Trauma bonding looks different for every couple. Both of you are somewhere on the trauma spectrum of fight, flight, freeze, or fawn, but rarely at the same point at the same time, leading to destructive patterns of behavior. This may appear as:

- Obsessing over the details of the affair for longer than nine months after it was initially discovered.
- Swinging between wanting a divorce and wanting to stay together.
- Continuing to argue over the same problems.

- Hiding your relationship from other people, so they don't judge you for being together.
- Breaking promises to yourself or your partner but still thinking things will improve.
- Feeling close and connected one minute and then being overwhelmed by painful memories the next.

If you recognize you and your partner in the above list, don't feel ashamed or that there's something wrong with you. Instead, start to think about how you can break these cycles. You may decide you want to work with a therapist to get professional support to lay down new patterns of behavior.

Ask yourself whether the way you discuss the affair is helping you figure things out or making things worse. While it is important to talk about it regularly in the aftermath of an affair, it's also important for the cheating spouse to step up and be the protector of the relationship during this period. Both of you should be curious about this negative cycle and what you can do differently since you're both responsible for laying down new ways of doing things and being together.

THE IMPORTANCE OF EMPATHY

As you move toward being able to forgive your partner, developing empathy is key.

Empathy is not:

- Apologizing without meaning it.
- Feeling sorry for your partner.
- Trying to change their situation.
- Giving advice or offering solutions.
- Justifying what you did.

Instead, it is:

- Identifying with their pain.
- Putting yourself in their position.
- Feeling compassion for their pain.
- Trying to experience their feelings or thoughts.
- Understanding their viewpoint.

When you can be empathic toward someone else, we experience their pain as our own. We break down the walls between us and see the other person as a human being—just like us. Empathy may seem to be a soft option, yet it's incredibly powerful in its effect on us.

Empathy is a skill that can be learned. After an affair, it's natural to emotionally disconnect from your partner, which results in you losing empathy for them and often yourself as well. You stop caring about your happiness and theirs, opening the doors to a cycle of self-destruction.

What's more, it's normal to want to save someone from painful emotions. But when we don't let people feel what they're feeling, it can make them feel like we're invalidating their experience. Allow them to feel sad, angry, depressed, and hopeless—but support them through it.

A simple way to understand empathy is to think about the feeling behind the story someone is telling you and then try to recall a time when you had a similar feeling. The most important thing here is the emotion, yet most of us fixate on the story and ignore the emotions. Sitting with someone who is suffering is incredibly difficult, but it's the only way you're going to be able to understand their experience and heal your relationship.

When you talk about the affair, try to focus on how your spouse is feeling. If they say something factually inaccurate, e.g., accusing you of calling your lover every day when it was really every other day, resist the temptation to correct them and instead consider what they're telling you about their feelings. Put an emotional response ahead of a factual response, and you will find yourselves growing closer as a couple.

This kind of communication takes practice, so be patient with each other as you establish this new way of doing things.

ESTABLISHING NEW BOUNDARIES

Boundaries help set what you expect from your relationship, defining your personal rules and needs. If your partner crosses a boundary, they're betraying your agreement with each other.

While boundaries may involve changing behavior, their real purpose is to protect your relationship. Your marriage is going to be different moving forward. There's no getting around that. But one of the ways in which you can feel secure in the future of your marriage is by setting and maintaining healthy boundaries, supporting both of you to feel you're doing the right thing by staying together.

First and foremost, the cheating partner has to stop communicating with the other person in any way. This includes text, email, phone, and social media. Turning your back on the other person and cutting them out of your life eliminates distractions and enables you to be completely focused on your spouse.

Next, the cheating partner needs to give their spouse complete access to their phone, email, or social media accounts. Normally, this would be a serious violation of privacy, but in the short term, this is essential to re-establish trust. Some people never take advantage of this access. The mere fact that the option is there is more than enough to reassure them, while others regularly check their spouse's accounts. It's entirely up to you what you feel is necessary.

You might like to:

- Have your partner's social media ID and password.
- Ask to see your partner's text messages at random times.
- Approve who your partner can privately message on social media.
- Ban the use of Snapchat or other platforms which automatically delete material.
- Link your partner's email account to yours.
- Get your partner always to keep their phone face up.
- Think about old behaviors and come up with alternatives, e.g., not taking calls out of earshot.

These measures won't last forever, but they'll help get your relationship back on an even keel. Revisit them after a month and see what you feel needs to stay in place a little longer.

When enforcing boundaries, try to do so from a place of love. They aren't there to get revenge on your spouse or try to control them. It's about reminding them that the way they've treated you isn't acceptable, and for the sake of your own self-respect and your marriage, you won't let their behavior continue. They then have two choices: either do whatever is necessary to respect your boundaries or continue to put their own needs first. If the latter is the case, you'll need to be prepared to do what it takes to maintain the boundary or make the difficult decision to walk away.

EXERCISES

Create a transparency plan

A transparency plan is your personal roadmap to re-establishing trust. This should be driven by the betraying partner as part of their attempt to make amends.

Start by identifying all the areas of your life you need to be open about. This might include:

- Work
- Social life
- Church
- Alone time
- Hobbies
- Family time
- Online/social media
- Email
- Financial accounts
- Electronic devices

Consider how you interact in these different areas and any others you can think of. So, you might write out your work hours and where you are when you're at work. (Home, office, traveling, etc.) List your regular social interactions and activities. Describe how often you check your phone and what you do when you're on it. You get the idea.

Include in this list where you had contact with your lover. So, you might have met your lover on a Friday afternoon when you were supposed to be in a meeting, emailed them from a secret account, and saw them when you said you were going to the gym, etc.

Once you've outlined your activities in every area of your life, the next step is to define what transparency will look like for you in each of those areas. For example, you might decide to let your spouse know about your daily plans. If those plans change, you will immediately tell your spouse. If your lover tries to contact you, you will let your spouse know, and you will also tell your spouse if you see your lover, even if it's just driving past them.

Then go through each area you've listed out and detail how you will be transparent about your activities. There will inevitably be opportunities for you to cheat again, so you need to be clear about what you're doing to remove that temptation.

For example, you might share your work schedule with your spouse and make sure you never have a meeting with someone of the opposite gender by yourself. You will let your spouse know your travel plans and agenda, calling as soon as you arrive or promptly communicating any delays or changes. You might look for other ways of entertaining yourself that don't involve your phone. You might include your spouse in your social activities or develop friendships with other married couples who are dedicated to their relationship. If you have any friends who are being unfaithful, cut them out of your life. That way, they can't tempt you to emulate them.

Once you've drafted your transparency plan, talk about it with your spouse. This might be a difficult conversation as you negotiate these new boundaries, but it's important you try to keep your focus on this new agreement rather than getting defensive or angry. You may like to have this discussion in front of your therapist or an impartial observer.

Ask your spouse for their thoughts and feedback on the plan. They may have ideas they need you to incorporate or suggestions on how you could do things differently. Work on a final version of the plan together so that you're both happy with it. When you've agreed on your transparency plan, it's a good idea to print out a copy for each of you so that you both know the new expectations and boundaries.

Create your own three-circle plan

The three-circle plan was originally developed by 12-step recovery groups but is now a common tool used in couples therapy. It encourages the unfaithful partner to look at wanted and unwanted behaviors, so they can put their focus on actions that support their relationship rather than undermine it.

Every couple's circles will be different, so be honest when creating yours, so it reflects your personal triggers and values.

Inner circle

Your inner circle contains behaviors you need to stop without question. Engaging in these actions means you've fallen back into your old negative ways and requires a re-evaluation of your boundaries and recovery.

The characteristics of inner circle actions include:

- You struggle to stop even though you want to.
- You hide them.
- You know there would be negative consequences if your spouse found out.
- They help you avoid negative feelings.
- They don't contribute to intimacy with your partner.
- They make you lose self-respect.

Things in your inner circle might include:

- Meeting or contacting your former lover.
- Going to a strip club.
- Watching porn.
- Going out with an opposite-sex co-worker.
- Sending texts, emails, messages, etc., with sexual innuendo to someone of the opposite sex.

Some couples like to have two categories of inner circle behavior—relapses and slips. A slip would be a one-off mistake that the person recognizes and immediately reaches out for help to prevent it from happening. While this is serious, it's not as bad as a relapse which involves falling back into old negative patterns. You may find there are some actions in your inner circle you consider to be so serious that one incidence would qualify as a relapse.

If you decide to take this approach, be aware that sometimes the unfaithful partner will depict a relapse as a slip, playing word games to cover up the fact that they are sliding back into dangerous territory. So, if you're noticing a few slips, consider whether the partner is genuinely committed to doing the inner work to restore the relationship.

Middle circle

These are borderline behaviors that may or may not be appropriate but have the potential to lead to an affair or other inner circle behaviors. Examples of this are:

- Spending too much time away from home.
- Spending too much time online playing games or browsing social media.
- Working late.
- Socializing alone.
- Procrastination.
- Resentment.

Middle circle behaviors can be dangerous because they may not be viewed as seriously as inner circle ones, so it's therefore okay to engage in them occasionally. Occasionally then becomes regularly, and before you know it, you're back to where you started. Monitor the frequency of middle circle behaviors so changes can be made before they become a problem.

Outer circle

This is where you list out the healthy behaviors which should be encouraged. This might be:

- Spending time as a couple.
- Spending time with family and friends.
- Regular sex.
- Talking with each other.
- Texting each other regularly.
- Going to therapy.
- Going to church.
- Making amends.
- Having an accountability partner.
- Journaling.
- Working through the exercises in this book.

Once you've agreed on your three circles, you might like to create a visual depiction of them that you can display somewhere you'll see them regularly. This can empower the unfaithful spouse to spot the danger signs before they get into trouble.

Agree that slips or relapses should be shared promptly, within 24–48 hours. This gives the unfaithful partner the opportunity to get support from an appropriate source and advice on the best way to communicate the details to their spouse.

In this chapter, we looked at accountability and empathy. You learned:

- How to take responsibility for your actions.
- How to be accountable for your actions.
- How to know if your spouse is likely to cheat again.
- The importance of empathy.
- How you can establish healthy boundaries for a stronger relationship in the future.

In the next chapter, we're going to look at the most important factor for the future of your relationship: restoring trust.

6

RESTORING TRUST

"I just don't think I can trust him again." Rebecca broke down in tears, and I handed her some tissues. She'd recently found out her husband was having an affair and didn't know how to cope. "I keep asking myself if I hadn't seen that text if he'd ever have told me. I simply don't see how I can trust another word that comes out of that man's mouth."

"I understand," I said. "But it's early days. The first question you need to be asking isn't *how can I trust him,* but *do I want to stay with him*? Everything else comes after that."

"I think I do." She sniffed. "I mean, we've got children together, a home, a life . . . At least I thought we did."

"That's a start." I smiled. "If you think you want to stay with him, then it's worth giving your marriage a shot. Trust—

once broken—is very hard to fix. Right now, the idea of trusting your husband again might feel impossible, but you can do it. It's going to take time. It's a process, and you can't rush it. If you try and push ahead before you're ready, you could undo all your hard work. But you—and your husband—are willing to devote time and energy to healing your relationship. There will come a day when you know you trust him again. Would you like to see that day?"

Rebecca thought for a moment. "Yes. I really think I would."

THE VALUE OF TRUST

Trust is probably the most important element of a healthy relationship. Once it's gone, it takes far more time, patience, and work to restore it than it did to build it in the first place. But you *can* get it back if you're both motivated enough.

Trust can be broken in many different ways. Obviously, if your partner cheats, that will destroy your trust, but it can also break down if one partner is manipulating situations to suit themselves; holding back on sharing their feelings with their spouse; being unreliable; breaking promises; or keeping secrets.

Trust is when you can believe that someone has positive motives toward you and will be able (or at least try) to support your needs. You can't make someone trust you. They have to decide that you're worthy of trust.

Trust doesn't mean you have to share absolutely every little thing about your life. It's normal to keep some thoughts, feelings, and experiences to yourself. Likewise, you don't have to have access to each other's finances, devices, or social media accounts. The whole point of trust is that you don't feel the need to check up on your partner. You have faith in them and are able to discuss whatever you need.

REBUILDING TRUST

Whether you can rebuild your trust in each other depends on both of you. The one who broke the trust needs to prove they will be honest moving forward, while the one who has been betrayed needs to choose to trust again. In the early days following the discovery of an affair, this might feel impossible, which is why the important thing to consider now isn't whether you think you can trust but whether you feel you want to continue with the relationship. Trust can come later.

If you want to stay in the relationship, these are some things you need to consider on your journey back to trust:

- **You must have respect.** While it's understandable you might feel like lashing out, you both need to have respect for each other in your interactions, regardless of how angry or sad you're feeling.
- **You need open communication.** You're going to have some difficult conversations in the months

ahead with some painful emotions arising as a consequence. You both need to process these through healthy, constructive dialog.

- **You need to be willing to be vulnerable.** When we trust someone, we allow ourselves to be emotionally vulnerable. It's going to take a while before you can let your guard down again, but eventually, you're going to need to be vulnerable again.
- **You should try to understand the reasons behind the affair.** This can be difficult when you're the one who's been betrayed. What happened was far from okay. But once you know the reasons for their straying, you can decide whether you're capable of rebuilding trust.
- **You should understand the difference between blind trust and mindful trust.** Right now, it's going to be almost impossible to trust completely and unconditionally. You'll need to reassure yourself that your partner is worthy of trust. Mindful trust means you examine your partner's words and deeds and give trust only if it's earned.
- **You should find the balance between giving and receiving.** In a healthy relationship, both partners benefit equally. Immediately after an affair, it's natural for the one who was betrayed to feel like the other needs to go to great lengths to prove their commitment and show their regret. This is an imbalance that can be constructive in the early

stages of recovery but, in the long run, is unsustainable. If the one who cheated is expected to always be the one to make all the effort, eventually, they'll start feeling like they're not respected and not in a partnership.

- **You need to forgive but not forget.** Just because you reach a place where you can forgive your partner doesn't mean you have to forget all about it. Forgiveness simply means you've decided to let go of negative thoughts toward the person who hurt you, regardless of whether they deserve it or not.
- **You should try to stay focused on the present.** The affair is likely to be dominating your thoughts for a long time. Acknowledge these feelings and talk about them with your partner, but also recognize that they're a response to something from the past that has given you fears for the future. At some point, you'll need to keep your focus on the present moment, which is all any of us have. Trust comes from what's happening right now, not what's happened in the past or might happen in the future.

It's possible your partner may make a mistake or two on the road to recovery. If they own up to it and you still have love and commitment for each other, working on your trust will strengthen your relationship. However, if you know you'll never be able to fully trust your partner, or they continue to behave deceitfully or don't take responsibility for their actions, it is probably better to decide to move forward separately.

GOTTMAN'S TRUST REVIVAL METHOD

The Gottman's Trust Revival Method is a three-step program developed by a counselor to help couples recover from infidelity. The three steps are atone, attune, and attach.

Atone

In this phase, it is the cheater's duty to accept responsibility without condition and make amends. They need to deal with any repercussions without becoming defensive, making excuses or retaliating.

This is usually the most difficult period. The betrayed partner has had their trust shattered and will be frequently triggered. They will be hurt and angry and bring up the cheating a lot. It may feel like things will never get better—but they will if you persevere.

According to Gottman's method, the offender should simply accept full responsibility for the affair and apologize whenever the affair is brought up. This can be tough, especially when you're in the throes of an argument, but if you can do this consistently and gradually, the affair will lose its grip on your relationship.

At the same time, the one who was betrayed needs to be open to forgiving their partner. When the betrayer is visibly making an effort, accepting responsibility, and being transparent in their actions, it's your role to acknowledge their efforts and forgive them.

Attune

Once you've reached a point where you think you can forgive, your attention can turn to building a new relationship. Both of you should recognize that you had needs that were not being met, and your old way of being together had some problems. This is the time to tackle those problems and find better strategies for supporting each other.

Attunement is the willingness and ability to respect and appreciate your partner's inner world. Sharing your vulnerabilities means neither of you will feel lonely or invisible.

One way of doing this is to set aside some time every day to check in with each other and ask how things are going. Try to avoid "you" statements, replacing them with "I feel" statements instead. For example, instead of saying, "You're selfish," say, "I feel sad and abandoned when you go out with your friends instead of taking me out." If you notice the other partner seems upset about something, ask open-ended questions which don't come with any assumptions. So rather than asking, "What have I done to annoy you now?" switch it with "You look upset. What's wrong?" This helps you avoid passive aggression or making little digs at each other all the time.

Taking the time to attune to each other pulls you closer together and helps you rebuild trust.

Attach

The final step involves sex. When one spouse has had a physical affair, it has a major impact on your sex life. The one who was betrayed may find it hard to be physically intimate without thinking about their spouse being with someone else. If your relationship is going to have a future, you both need to enjoy your sex life.

During the attunement stage, you started having more productive and personal conversations. Now you should start talking about sex to rekindle the passion between you.

Ask your partner questions so you can learn more about their sexual preferences.

You might like to start with:

- What's an instant turn-on for you?
- What fantasies do you have?
- How can I make sex more romantic for you?
- Where do you most like to be touched?
- How would you like me to initiate sex?
- What's your favorite position?
- What's your favorite part of my body?
- Where do you most like to be kissed?
- Would you be open to using sex toys?

Having open communication about everything, including sex, will help you get back to enjoying each other in the bedroom, bringing you both together. What's more, most affairs occur because one partner was getting their needs met. It has little to do with lust. If your relationship is healthy and you have open communication, there is no drive to get your physical needs met elsewhere.

WHY WOULD YOU WANT TO REBUILD TRUST?

This is a very personal question only you can answer. It may be as simple as you still love your spouse, even though you don't love their behavior. Maybe you have a family together. Whatever your reasons for staying, **you** have to be the one to want to do the work. If you stay in your marriage because someone else wants you to, you'll eventually end up resenting your partner and may even have an affair yourself because your needs aren't being met.

If you're following the processes outlined in this book and the spouse who cheated is noticeably making an effort, you're in a good place to start trusting. There are no guarantees in this life. Nobody can promise they won't ever hurt you again, but if you're communicating and are looking to do things differently in the future, the chances are massively reduced that anyone will want to cheat.

FORGIVENESS AFTER AN AFFAIR

We've mentioned forgiveness a lot in this book. Forgiveness is such a powerful tool that you have to take control of your feelings and responses. However, you will have noticed that I've advised against apologizing too soon. This is because if you apologize immediately after an affair, you're not in a position to fully appreciate the damage your behavior has done, rendering the apology meaningless. What's more, the more an unfaithful partner apologizes, the more they expect that to be enough for their spouse to forgive and move on. As we've already seen, a lot more work needs to be done to reach that point. An apology by itself won't cut it, and the more someone is pressured to forgive, the more it becomes a Band-Aid that doesn't heal anything and leaves the door wide open for negative patterns to continue.

It is easier to forgive your partner for an affair if you both use this experience as an opportunity to bring you closer than you've ever been. You'll need to look at the vulnerabilities in your relationship that allowed an affair to happen in the first place. This will involve both of you accepting how you contributed to exposing your marriage to a threat. You should both open up about how you've been feeling in the past, which may have been going on for years. Then you can forgive each other—and yourself.

There are three stages to the process of forgiveness:

1. Restoring your faith in your partner. This means moving from "How could you cheat on me?" to "How did we drift so far apart?"
2. The one who was cheated on lets go of their pain and anger, and you both consider what happened to get you to this place.
3. You resolve ongoing issues, change how you view your spouse and restore your trust. You use the affair as a mechanism for you to build a stronger, more intimate relationship.

Try thinking of the affair as the straw which broke the back of an already unstable marriage. Tough questions and discussions around the state of your relationship are what will get you on the path of healing and forgiveness.

Rather than asking, "Why . . . why did you do this?" think about questions starting with how, what, or when. For example:

- How did your affair make you feel? How was it different to how you feel about me? Did you feel you got more love from them? More attention?
- Have you ever felt like that in our marriage, and when did you stop feeling that way?
- What specifically changed your feelings?

- What was the main difference between your relationship with your lover and our marriage?
- What do we need to do differently in the future?

Rebuilding trust means you need to honestly examine the existing weaknesses in your marriage and whether you really do want to deal with them. Bringing empathy into this process is also helpful. Understanding how your partner feels and recognizing those feelings in yourself can bring you closer.

THE THREE PHASES OF AFFAIR RECOVERY

1. Hurt partner stabilization

This occurs in the immediate aftermath of an affair when you both try to make sense of what happened. We've covered a lot about what to do during this stage, which involves full disclosure, setting new boundaries and deciding what you want to do moving forward.

Once the person who was betrayed feels secure enough to progress with the relationship, you can move on to the second phase.

2. Epiphany

This is when you work together to discover how the affair was able to happen. By having the kinds of conversations detailed in this chapter, you'll have a moment of realization that enables you to view the infidelity from a new, deeper perspective. You continue to discuss the vulnerabilities in your marriage and what you both did to contribute to the disconnect you experienced. This can be particularly hard if you were the one who was cheated on—you've been betrayed, and now you've got to accept you contributed to the situation? But this stage isn't about blame. It's about taking this opportunity to do some self-reflection and choose to do things differently in the future.

3. Phoenix

By this phase, you've both decided to recommit to your marriage. You may like to do a vow renewal or commitment ceremony to mark this breakthrough. You've recovered from the damage done by the affair, and you're rebuilding trust every day. You're working together to create a new, stronger marriage.

Right now, that moment might feel a long way away. That's okay. You'll get there when you're ready.

HOW MINDFULNESS CAN HELP YOU MOVE PAST BETRAYAL

Mindfulness is increasingly popular as a therapeutic tool because of its versatility. Mindfulness techniques can help you be more compassionate toward yourself and those around you. What's more, they can help you to be more forgiving—extremely important for infidelity recovery.

Mindfulness brings with it many benefits. The most important for infidelity is the ability to:

- Impartially observe your thoughts, feelings, perceptions, and sensations.
- Describe your experience.
- Act with awareness and consciousness.
- Be nonjudgmental of the current moment.
- Be nonreactive to what's happening, avoiding knee-jerk reactions.

Using mindfulness following an affair can help you avoid being overwhelmed by negative emotions. You can practice it by:

- Allowing yourself to sit with any negative emotions rather than fighting or repressing them.
- Relieving physical symptoms with stress management tools, such as focusing on your breathing or taking a walk in nature.

- Consciously deciding to forgive yourself and your partner.
- Viewing your partner with compassion. Acknowledge that they were acting from a place of pain and suffering and view them as simply being human, as vulnerable as you.

EXERCISES

Mindfulness practice

If you find yourself struggling with negative, painful thoughts, use mindfulness to reframe them.

Pause, close your eyes, and take a moment to focus on your breathing. After a few inhalations and exhalations, turn your attention to your sense of hearing. Observe what you can hear without judgment. After a few moments, turn your attention to your sense of smell. Notice if you can smell anything or the absence of smell without judgment. After a few moments, turn your attention to your sense of taste. Do you taste anything, maybe an aftertaste of something you ate or drank earlier? Consider your current experience without judgment. Next, turn your attention to your sense of touch. What can you feel against your body? Your clothes? A chair, couch, or bed? A breeze? Really tune into how you're feeling without judgment. Finally, open your eyes and gaze around you without judgment. Can you see anything you didn't notice earlier? If you're in a familiar place, can you spot something new?

Just being present in this way supports you to understand that your thoughts are not you. They are simply thoughts and can change in an instant.

Recovery check-in

You should establish regular recovery check-ins with each other. You might like to start doing this daily and slowly cut it back to weekly. Treat this as seriously as you would any business meeting and put the onus on the unfaithful partner to initiate it.

Actively listen to what your partner is telling you, keeping your focus on what they're saying rather than what you want to say in response.

Start with the unfaithful partner giving a fidelity report, such as "I've been completely faithful since our last check-in." Then the pair of you should share positive thoughts about each other, such as how you've noticed the other one investing in the relationship, things they've done for you, things they've said or attributes you appreciate.

Check in about your feelings. How are you feeling right now? What makes you feel safe or close to your partner? What undermines that feeling of safety or closeness? You may have more than one feeling, and that's okay. Go into detail about all of them.

Close by sharing what you've been doing to stay on track and work on your relationship. This might be books you've read, podcasts you've listened to, therapy sessions, etc., as well as any insights or breakthroughs you've experienced.

In this chapter, you learned:

- Why trust is so important.
- What you can do to rebuild trust.
- How you can use Gottman's trust revival method.
- How you can be ready to forgive.
- The three phases of affair recovery.
- How you can use mindfulness to help you cope with the impact of an affair.

We also discussed the importance of physical intimacy. Since this is such an important subject, we're going to devote the whole of the next chapter to this.

7

SEX AND INTIMACY

"It's really embarrassing," Bernice said.

"That's okay. Take your time." I subtly moved the box of tissues I kept on my desk, so it was within reach. "Whatever you've got to say, it'll be nothing I haven't heard before. Nothing shocks me."

Bernice smiled weakly. "It's about our sex life. Before I found out about his affair, it was like we couldn't keep our hands off each other. There was such a spark between us. I guess I should have known something was up when he started making excuses for not wanting to make love to me."

She sniffed and reached for a tissue. I waited for her to start talking again after she dabbed at her eyes.

"We split up for a couple of months after I found out, but we missed each other too much, so we got back together. The problem is that I hate having sex with him. It's like his penis is tainted. I can't stop thinking about all the things he was doing with *her.* I asked him to wait for us to rebuild our trust before we started having sex again, but then I thought that if we weren't sleeping with each other, he'd go off and find someone else to meet his needs. It's been so hard. I want to have sex with him again, but only when I feel ready, but right now, I don't. I just don't."

Bernice's story is nothing new. Many people struggle to enjoy the kind of sex they had before an affair came to light. There's no doubt that sex brings couples together as much as it can drive them apart, but if you're going to bring back the physical aspect of your relationship, you'll need to re-establish your intimacy and friendship.

The first thing you need to do to bring more intimacy into your relationship is to increase the amount of time you spend together. This underlies all your other efforts. When couples start to look into the reasons for an affair, lack of shared quality time is often one of the biggest factors. Many couples find that life gets in the way—kids, careers, screen-time, social obligations—and making time for each other ends up falling to the bottom of the list. If you have children, many evenings and weekends get occupied with children's activities, leaving little time for you as a couple.

It's time to say no. Your children will survive if they're not doing a class every day. It's time to put your marriage first. Your children will benefit more from having happy parents than from another sporting activity.

You'll need to plan activities for your marriage with the same diligence you do for your children. Rather than waiting for an opportunity to arise for you to spend time together, actively schedule time to do something together. Being spontaneous means you hope you'll spend time together—and may end up disappointed. Planning to hang out means it happens because you've consciously decided to make it happen.

It may be a while since you've spent time together, so here are some ideas for shared activities you might enjoy:

- Play board games.
- Do something together for the first time.
- Cook a meal together.
- Go to a museum, art gallery, or lecture.
- Read a book to each other.
- Go to a dance class.
- Go to a gig, concert, or movie.
- Take an adult education class together.
- Join a book club.
- Work in the garden.
- Check out local sites of interest together.

HAVING INTIMATE CONVERSATIONS

It may be a while since you've opened up to each other. Heck, you may never have had a truly intimate conversation with each other. I want to take a moment to give you some guidelines to having genuinely productive conversations.

The **only** goal to an intimate conversation is to understand the other. Forget problem-solving or advising. This can only come after someone feels understood. There are three things you need to bear in mind when you have an intimate conversation:

1. Put your feelings into words

This is easier for some people than others, but when you can find the right images, phrases, metaphors, etc., to express how you feel, you reveal more than just your current state of being. The words you choose speak volumes about whom you are, making your conversations deeper, more intense and intimate.

2. Ask open questions

Encourage your partner to open up further by asking open questions that promote further discussion and get them to give more detail. You could ask targeted questions like: "What's the worst-case scenario here?" or statements to obtain more details like: "I'd love to hear the story behind that."

3. Express empathy

We've discussed the importance of empathy earlier in this book. In these kinds of conversations, showing empathy means demonstrating that you understand the other person's experience. It's important to note that you may not agree with their experience. You may recollect things differently or have a different perspective, and that's okay. When you're being empathetic, you're accepting that your partner's perceptions, thoughts, feelings, and needs are just as valid as yours, even if they may vary.

REBUILDING YOUR SEXUAL RELATIONSHIP

Once you've started to regain your sense of intimacy, you can start to heal your sexual relationship. There are three phases to this recovery process:

1. The crisis phase

This is the period immediately after the discovery of the affair. This is when you'll be feeling emotionally unstable and struggling to practice self-care. You're likely to be arguing a lot yet may well be having more sex than ever. This doesn't mean you've forgiven your partner, but this form of sex is a way of trying to connect and re-establish your claim to your partner's affections.

This can be a confusing time for both of you as you try to build a new relationship and discover who you both are.

Others may find that they're not having any sex at all. You may be feeling so angry and betrayed that you can't see yourself ever having sex again. If this is you, talk to your partner about your feelings. Let them know you're not ready to have sex and tell them what you are comfortable with, such as cuddling in bed or holding hands in public.

Slow down, and don't put any pressure on yourself to have sex before you feel ready. This phase will pass.

2. The insight phase

In this phase, you move from blame and recrimination into curiosity about how this happened and why. The focus is on understanding each other and building empathy.

This is when you can discover what real intimacy will be like between you moving forward.

You can start exploring each other erotically again. You'll be building a new sex life together, trying new things as you give your relationship another chance. Some couples find their sex is better than ever following this phase.

3. The vision phase

This is when you decide if you're going to stay together and what that will look like. This will include your sex life. If you ignore this aspect of your relationship and simply focus on avoiding conflict, you'll end up as good roommates, but you won't be in love anymore—which is the death of a relationship.

Building this erotic connection will take work, just like all other aspects of your marriage. But it's work that will pay off in dividends.

THE IMPORTANCE OF SEX

Humans are sexual creatures. We are driven to have sex as much as we are to eat or drink. It is a basic human need.

However, just as our desire for food can be affected by our emotions, our sex drive can also be influenced by our mood. Stress, anxiety, and depression can all negatively affect our desire for sex, although, in some people, they can increase the sex drive as a way of generating more of the feel-good hormones which accompany sex. The relationship between your sex drive and your emotions is complex and nuanced, which is why you need to devote specific care and attention to rebuilding your sexual connection following an affair.

Restoring sexual intimacy

The affair will have a major impact on your sex life. If you fall into the camp that has more sex, understand that this isn't necessarily a good thing because that sex is being fueled by intense pain as the betrayed partner is mentally comparing themselves to the other lover. If you're avoiding sex, you'll be wondering how you can begin to physically connect again.

- **Avoid comparing yourself to the other lover.** It may be difficult, but don't beat yourself up wondering how you compare to the other person. We have our strengths and weaknesses and comparing yourself to someone else will only leave you falling short. Instead, turn your attention to yourself and how you can feel loved and wanted by your spouse for who you are.
- **Move past feelings of guilt, shame, and unworthiness.** If you're the one who cheated, you may find it hard to overcome your feelings of having betrayed your spouse. You may also be grieving the loss of your other relationship. This is perfectly normal—it can take at least six months of no contact with your lover to really move past them. Accept your feelings for what they are, but work to get past them—with the help of a therapist if need be.
- **Recognize that it's the responsibility of you both to restore sexual intimacy.** It really does take two to

tango. It's not an issue for one of you. This is an issue for you **both**. Sex and intimacy serve many purposes, including healing, comfort, reconciliation, building self-esteem, expressing love, building bonds, relaxation, feeling attractive, and making your partner happy. This is for the benefit of both of you.

- **Understand that you should have sex as soon as possible after an affair.** (But without either partner feeling like they're being forced into it.) As we've just mentioned, sex serves a variety of purposes which are all key to a healthy relationship. The sooner you can restore sexual activity, the sooner the healing can start.
- **Do not mistake sex for forgiveness.** While you may be ready to have sex, this doesn't mean everything is forgiven. A lot of work needs to be done for you to repair your marriage. That will take time, but it's difficult to heal if you're not enjoying sexual intimacy.
- **Start discussing sex openly and honestly.** This may have been a taboo subject for you until now, so you may feel you need the support of a therapist to start having productive conversations about sex. As a general guideline, don't talk about problems with intimacy while you're trying to be intimate. Simply hold each other and don't pressure anyone. Talk about it later when you can talk about it in a more objective manner.

- **Focus on lovemaking.** There are many, many different ways to enjoy your partner sexually, from sweet, tender lovemaking to passionate, dirty jungle sex. In a healthy marriage, however you express yourself sexually (with consent) is fine. But in the immediate aftermath of an affair, it's better to keep your focus on lovemaking while you work to restore your trust.
- **Be open to doing things with your spouse you did with your lover if that's what they want.** It's important for the cheater to be sensitive to the needs of their spouse so they can feel sexually attractive. If they want to explore their sexuality in a way you did with your lover, be open to meeting their needs.

The simple truth is that if there's no sexuality or intimacy in your marriage, your marriage won't be able to go the distance.

How you can reconnect sexually

You may be struggling to start having sex with your partner. You may find it difficult to even talk about the subject. Yet sex is a key part of any relationship. You may have an opinion of your spouse's sexuality that has no basis in reality. Or you may have thoughts and desires you feel embarrassed or ashamed to share with your partner.

However, you simply can't know what your spouse really thinks if you don't talk to them! This lack of transparency is one of the things that can lead to an affair, as the frustrated spouse looks for other outlets for their sexual needs.

Here are some ways you can start rebuilding your sex life:

- **Intimacy monologs.** We often have superficial conversations where we talk but don't actually communicate. Small talk is fine, but if you only ever have shallow conversations, you'll never experience intimacy. One way of doing this is to take it in turns to talk about your thoughts, needs, and wants without interruption. Share something you've never shared with anyone. Open up to your partner and while your partner is talking, listen to what they're actually saying without thinking about what you're going to say next.
- **Intimacy interviews.** Another way to get closer to your partner is to ask them questions about subjects to which you don't know the answer. And if you think you know the answer, ask them anyway—you may be surprised by the reply! Examples include:

    ○ What would your perfect day look like?
    ○ What are the most important things on your bucket list?
    ○ What do you like most about our relationship?
    ○ What would you like to do but have been too afraid to try?

  - What's one thing you would like to change about yourself?
  - What are three things you admire about yourself/me?
  - What's your favorite memory from all our dates?
  - If you could be any movie or book character, who would you be and why?
  - If you had enough money to start a business, what business would you start?
  - Which of your parents are you most like and why?
  - What would a perfect date with me look like?

- **Sexual touch.** You should decide on a way to communicate when doing these exercises. You could use verbal cues, ratings or taking your partner's hand so you can control the way they touch you. Do them when you're both rested and have plenty of time.

Take turns being the giver and receiver in the three stages of this exercise:

1. Take turns touching each other's bodies all over with the exception of the genitals and breasts. Take 15 minutes to explore your partner's body before swapping. This stage isn't about eliciting sexual arousal but rather being mindful of the sensations created, describing them in a nonjudgmental fashion.

The person touching should be guided by their intuition and curiosity to decide where and how to touch. The person being touched should give feedback on where to touch.

2. Expand this practice to include the breasts and genitals. However, don't start with these areas—explore the rest of the body first. Again, the focus should be on the physical sensations rather than intentionally arousing the other person. Avoid actual intercourse.
3. Now engage in mutual touching. This mimics a more natural way of physically interacting while you keep your attention on your partner's body rather than your own response. Full intercourse is still to be avoided.
4. After a few sessions of the first three stages, you can move to having the woman sitting on top, initially without penetration. In this position, you can rub your genitals against each other before slowly moving to inserting the penis into the vagina. All the while, keep your focus on the physical sensations and whether they're pleasurable, being open to going back to an earlier stage if either partner becomes uncomfortable. While orgasm isn't the goal here, if you both want to progress to that, feel free.

- **Nonsexual touching.** Nonsexual touching is just as important as sex, if not more so when it comes to building intimacy. However, in some couples, nonsexual touching is neglected out of a fear that any touch will be interpreted as an invitation for sex when they're not in the mood. If a couple only touches, hugs, or kisses each other as a prelude to sex, the passion in a relationship withers and dies. Nonsexual touching can be as simple as holding hands, cuddling or sitting close enough that your arms or legs touch while you're doing something like watching a movie. It's any touch that isn't intended to lead to sex. If you're not used to nonsexual touching, you might like to try a 3-minute hug. Set a timer for 3 minutes and simply hold each other. It might feel awkward at first, but you'll soon relax into each other. Or you could try kissing for 30 seconds. Most of the time, we default to a quick peck on the lips. Actively kissing for longer will make you feel closer, and it's such a simple practice.

- **Foreplay mapping.** When handled properly, the entire human body can be an erogenous zone. Take some time to explore some neglected parts of the body. Try giving your partner a head massage, kiss, lick, or nibble your partner's earlobes, or caress gentle circles around your partner's navel and lower stomach. Use your imagination as you discover there are no limits to what you can enjoy with your partner.

- **Create a sensual bedroom environment.** Transforming your bedroom into a space that is inviting and supports intimacy goes a long way to enhancing your sex life. Consider all five senses as you work on your bedroom. Clear out all the clutter, so the room is visually pleasing. You might like to clear out beneath the bed as a symbolic step toward clearing out anything which has been holding you back from expressing yourself sexually. Use candles to create a gentle mood. You could light scented candles or incense to make the room smell inviting. Put on music you both like which supports the mood you're trying to create. Turn off the TV, your phone, and any other devices that might interrupt you with beeps and noises. Have some massage oil next to the bed as a way of encouraging both nonsexual and sexual touch.

Other ways to reignite passion

- **Change how you initiate sex.** It's easy to fall into a rut, push your partner away or come on too strong. Try not to criticize each other and switch things up. If you're the one waiting for the other to make a move, practice initiating sex more often. If you're the one who usually starts things, think of different ways to tell your partner you find them sexy without making it sound like a come-on.

- **Hold hands.** This simple practice can release oxytocin, one of the feel-good hormones. Physical affection can also lower levels of stress hormones, relaxing you even more.
- **Take your time.** Instead of jumping straight into sex, spend more time on foreplay. Allowing tension to build will make things all the more intense when you finally have intercourse.
- **Keep chores out of the bedroom.** Maintain a sense of intimacy by banning discussion of chores and relationship issues from the bedroom. Keep it as your sanctuary from the mundane world.
- **Make time for your partner.** Start dating. Flirt with each other. Have fun together. It's all a form of foreplay.
- **Be affectionate in your touch.** Give your partner a massage without it leading to sex. Touching your partner affectionately is a way of bringing you closer together and showing you care about them.
- **Be more emotionally vulnerable.** If you've been holding back about your sexual desires, now's the time to share your secret thoughts and fantasies with them.
- **Keep experimenting.** You have a lifetime to explore each other's bodies. We all change over time. Play around with different ways of giving your partner pleasure as a way of getting to know them better.

- **Vary the type of sex you have.** Sex falls on a spectrum of gentle, loving, and intimate, right through to kinky and 'dirty.' Mix up the kind of sex you have to avoid falling into a routine.
- **Make time for sex.** If you have to schedule it, schedule it. Carve out time in your diary for intimacy. Take time to set the mood beforehand. You don't have to go out to dinner. You could stay in, put on your favorite music, cook a favorite meal together and enjoy a bottle of wine before retiring to the bedroom.

The talking exercise

There are lots of practical exercises in this chapter, but I wanted to close with one of my favorite ways of enhancing intimacy—the talking exercise.

It's very simple: set a timer and talk about yourself nonstop without interruption for 20 minutes. This is something we often do naturally at the start of a relationship or when we have an affair, but it rarely happens in established long-term relationships. You may avoid doing this because you think your partner will think you're boring, selfish or narcissistic. Alternatively, you may worry about what your partner will do when you open yourself up and are vulnerable.

It's important to push through these fears. A lack of communication is frequently a reason for an affair. We all want to be known and loved for who we are.

Some conversation starters could include:

- Your earliest memories.
- Your experiences in specific school grades.
- Your first kiss/date/boy/girlfriend.
- Your happiest and worst birthday.
- Your favorite teacher.
- Your first job.
- Your parents' favorite and how you felt about that.
- Your favorite relative.
- Where you've lived.
- How you spent your allowance.
- The best day ever.
- What age you'd like to be.

Whatever subject you choose, the important thing is to share how it makes you feel. Feelings are how you intimately connect, and you should discuss and explore what you've said when your time is up.

This is most effective when you take turns on different days, so the spotlight can be completely on one person each time you do this exercise rather than thinking about what you want to say.

In this chapter, you learned:

- The importance of sex and intimacy.
- How to have intimate conversations.

- How to rebuild and restore your sexual relationship.
- Numerous ways to get your sex life back on track.

In the next chapter, we're going to look at what you can do to finally move forward from an affair to enjoy a brighter and better future.

8

MOVING FORWARD

One of my favorite stories is about Marie and Mark. Mark first discovered that Marie was cheating when he picked up her phone to look for a photo of the two of them and instead found rather intimate photos of another man. He confronted Marie, who immediately confessed that she'd been seeing her lover for a year.

Mark was devastated. A religious man who loved his wife and children more than anything, he wasn't ready to walk away from his vows.

He immediately arranged for the pair of them to see me, both individually as a couple. They came to see me every week. Marie completely cut ties with her lover, which was what persuaded Mark that he'd made the right decision. Marie stopped lying, accepted responsibility for what she'd done and worked with her husband to rebuild their marriage.

Recently they had their last session with me, and this is what Mark had to say:

"I wouldn't say our marriage is perfect, but what marriage is? We're pretty close to being the Mark and Marie of the good old days, but better. Now, if either of us gets upset, we talk about how we feel. Marie is understanding when I talk about how her affair made me feel, and I don't really need to talk about it anymore. Although it was painful, I've forgiven her for what happened.

"I've learned to trust her again. Our sex life is great, and we're going on regular dates together. If we feel ourselves drifting apart, we talk about it and make an effort to reconnect. We both have our own social lives, but I know I can trust Marie. She's the love of my life, and although she made a big mistake, I wouldn't want to be without her."

Mark and Marie's story (and that of many of my clients) show that you *can* heal your relationship after an affair. As long as you're both willing and committed to rebuilding your marriage, you have a very good chance of finding your way back to each other.

UNDERSTANDING YOUR EMOTIONAL NEEDS

It is important that you both understand you and your partner's individual emotional needs. People change as they mature, and what worked for you in the past may not be working now. Maybe you're meeting your spouse's needs at your own expense. Perhaps you feel you can't talk about your needs. If you can't be clear about what you need from your partner, your relationship is at risk. If an affair isn't the wake-up call that you need to make a change, your relationship really is going to fail.

Some of the most common emotional needs include:

- **Admiration.** If you have a strong need for admiration, you may have been drawn to your spouse because of how they complimented or appreciated you. The problem with this need is that if it's not fed regularly, you can feel like your partner no longer admires you, whereas it may simply be that, over time, your partner has fallen out of the habit of complimenting you. If your partner needs admiration, make an effort to start telling them what you love about them again. A little goes a long way.
- **Family commitments.** When you have children, it changes things. You now have to take into consideration their needs as well as your own. There can be problems if the pair of you clash on how you're going to raise the children. If you can, talk

about your expectations before you have children. How much do you want to be involved in children's activities? What responsibilities are you both going to take on in caring for the children? How are you going to discipline them? If you already have children, you can still have these conversations. It's never too late to adjust what you're doing.

- **Affection.** In the last chapter, we discussed the need for intimacy and affection. This doesn't have to equate to sex. Holding hands, giving a back rub, going for a walk together, or snuggling up to watch a movie together, can all satisfy someone's need for affection.
- **Sex.** Again, the last chapter went into this in depth. Meeting each other's sexual needs is one of the most fundamental requirements of a healthy relationship.
- **Conversation.** The need for human connection through conversation extends beyond a relationship. We all need a range of people in our social circle to fulfill this need. However, you should be cautious of getting this need met outside of your marriage as a replacement for conversation with your spouse. This can easily lead to an emotional affair. Make time to simply talk with each other as part of your regular commitment to being with each other.
- **Companionship.** Again, there's nothing wrong with seeking this outside of your marriage, but you need to be careful of ending up spending more time with

people other than your spouse. Find activities you can both enjoy together, so you spend as much time with each other as you do with your friends. Your partner should always be the person you most want to hang around with.

- **Honesty and openness.** We all need honesty from our spouse, but some have a higher need for it than others. If you have a high need for honesty, you feel secure and close to your partner when your partner gives you accurate details about their thoughts, feelings, activities, plans, etc. Make sure you are open with each other—if one senses the other is keeping secrets, it can lead to paranoia and distrust, which will undermine all your hard work of repairing your relationship.
- **Physical attractiveness.** Most of us need to feel physically attracted to our partners. Our appearances change over time, and it's common for couples to feel like the other is neglecting their appearance and not making the same effort they used to. The trick to dealing with this is to work on your own self-esteem to keep yourself happy and healthy. You might like to work together to eat healthily and get exercise. If you place a particular emphasis on appearance, make sure your spouse knows about this and is happy to meet this need.
- **Financial support.** You may not have married for money, but financial security is important. If a life-

changing event occurs, such as redundancy or unemployment, money can impact your relationship. You may have different views about what constitutes financial support. One might be happy to have enough to get by while the other might have big ambitions. Your opinions about finances might change over the years. Money is the cause of many arguments between couples, and it's important to recognize that a need for financial stability and security is perfectly reasonable.

- **Domestic support.** We've come a long way since the days of women cleaning the home while the man goes out to work. It's more likely that a couple will need to find a way to balance domestic chores with other commitments, especially when children come along. Don't be afraid to regularly discuss how you divide up chores in a way you both feel is fair. If you find yourself being happy if your spouse takes on the task of cooking, cleaning, or childcare and get frustrated if they don't do those things, domestic support is an emotional need of yours and one you should talk about.

FORGIVENESS AND ACCEPTANCE

By now, you should be ready to forgive your spouse, accept what's happened, and move on to build a future together.

If you are the one who cheated, you should:

- Admit that what you did was wrong.
- Understand and empathize with the pain you caused.
- Take responsibility for your actions and make amends.
- Promise your partner you will try not to stray again.
- Apologize and ask for forgiveness.
- Forgive yourself.

If you are the one who was betrayed, you should:

- Acknowledge and talk through your pain and anger.
- Set clear boundaries and expectations for the future.
- Release any need to get back at your partner.
- Release any negative feelings of blame and resentment.
- Tell your partner you forgive them.
- Work toward reconciliation.

FORGIVENESS RITUALS AND CELEBRATIONS

There is a very human need to hold rituals to mark important milestones. The most common rituals are christenings, weddings, and funerals. But there are other occasions when they're appropriate—such as celebrating your commitment to staying together.

When you feel ready, you might like to hold some form of ritual or celebration. This might include symbolically getting rid of any items associated with the affair. Perhaps the cheater has kept cards or photos from their lover. You could set a date to ritually burn these together to symbolize your new start. Alternatively, you might like to hold a vow renewal ceremony. You could include your children and make it a large celebration, or you might like to do it privately in an intimate ceremony without any witnesses.

FORGIVENESS IS A JOURNEY

If you're struggling to forgive your spouse, consider whether you're a forgiving person. If you've never forgiven anyone, you're going to find it hard to forgive your partner for betraying your trust so badly.

Remember that forgiveness is a process. It doesn't have to happen all at once. You'll find that you gradually let go of transgressions over time which eventually adds up to an ability to move on rather than it being a major one-time event.

Just because you've forgiven an affair doesn't mean positive feelings will immediately come rushing in to chase away the negative ones. You'll still need to work on processing the hurt you've experienced. Forgiveness means you're willing to let go of the hold the past has over you, not that you're necessarily there yet. The past has happened and can't be undone. You're simply deciding to let it go.

Forgiveness doesn't mean your partner has to stop making an effort. The onus is on them to continue to prove their commitment to you and your marriage. They still have a responsibility to make amends and own their choices. The hard work still needs to be done to ensure it doesn't happen again.

Forgiveness doesn't mean you'll forget about the affair. In fact, it's good if you don't—that way, you'll both always have perspective on how far you've come and how much you've got to lose. But you can stop obsessing about it and let it be something that happened, but it's in the past now. If you've been putting all my recommendations in place, you'll find your relationship is all the stronger for it, so while nobody ever wants their spouse to cheat, you may reach a point where you view it as a positive thing because of how great your marriage is now.

Don't forgive until you're ready. This takes as long as it takes, and if you forgive because you think it's the right thing to do rather than because you're actually feeling it, you won't be able to dig deep and do the hard work required to heal your marriage. What's more, you'll end up resenting your partner because they'll think things are okay when they're really not.

If you're not ready to forgive even after doing all the work outlined in this book, you might want to consider getting professional help. A therapist can help you work through what's holding you back and support you to finally find peace with what went on—or leave the relationship if that's what's right for you.

Likewise, don't forgive your partner because you want the fighting to end. This will only brush your problems under the carpet. If you don't deal with the issues that got you to this place, those cycles will end up repeating. There are healthier ways to resolve conflict than arguing, and you can always find a therapist to help you talk things through.

DECIDING TO STAY TOGETHER

Eventually, there will come a point when you have to make a decision to stay with your partner and work things through or walk away. This isn't a decision that should be made lightly or quickly. It can take several months before you feel ready to properly recommit, and that's okay. But that time needs to come because, without a conscious decision to recommit, you can end up feeling stuck and emotionally distant, settling for a relationship that is unfulfilling for both of you.

You may need to sit and formally redefine your marriage to know exactly what you both want. Do you want a relationship that is better than before, or do you simply want to get through what's happened? Do you want to move forward together? What does that look like for you? Do you still want to remain in your marriage?

Only you can answer these questions. For some couples, it's better to go your separate ways. If you don't love, respect, or even like each other, you would be better off ending the marriage than continuing to be miserable.

But if you've worked through the exercises in this book and have come to the realization that you have something worth saving, you should have a clear idea of what went wrong and what you can do to avoid it happening again.

You don't have to make any big decisions right away. Take it step by step. You might like to commit to staying for the next three months and then review depending on whether you've seen any real change in your partner. You can examine the boundaries you put in place and consider adjusting them in light of how much your partner's done to make amends.

If you do decide to commit to staying, move forward with a plan for success. Identify your relationship's weaknesses and put strategies in place to compensate for them.

WAYS TO STAY COMMITTED TO YOUR MARRIAGE

- **Write a commitment statement.** This will outline the purpose and goal of your marriage. You might also include rules and boundaries to support your marriage.

- **Greet each other personally and physically every day.** Not only are hugs and kisses nice, but these little affectionate touches also reinforce your commitment to each other.
- **Talk about your hopes, dreams, and goals.** Talking about the future you're going to enjoy together will reinforce your current commitment.
- **Make time for each other.** Whether you go out on a date or just enjoy being together, regularly having quality time together reinforces your commitment to each other.
- **Be best friends.** Friendship makes for a happy and healthy marriage.
- **Do spiritual/religious activities together.** This can help bring you closer and strengthen your bonds.
- **Practice little acts of kindness.** Showing you've been thinking about your spouse is a simple way of demonstrating your respect and dedication to each other.

So there you have it. Well done for working your way through this book and taking the first step on the journey to recovering from betrayal. While you don't have an easy road ahead of you, if you're willing to do the hard work and push through the tough times, you can end up with a marriage that is stronger than ever.

In this chapter, you learned:

- All about your different emotional needs.
- How you can forgive and accept your spouse.
- Forgiveness rituals and celebrations you might like to do to mark your commitment to your marriage.
- Forgiveness is a journey. It's okay to take your time getting to a place of acceptance.
- Making a conscious decision to stay together.
- Ways you can reaffirm your decision to recommit.

I want to take a moment to congratulate you on working through this book. I can't promise you everything will be okay, but I do know that whatever happens, you'll be able to say you've done everything you could to work things out.

CONCLUSION

Whether you picked up this book because you've recently learned your spouse has had an affair or you've known for a while but haven't been able to figure out what to do to heal your relationship, you hold in your hands a powerful toolkit to get past the betrayal and rebuild your marriage.

It will take work from both of you. Remember—an affair is always the fault of the one who strayed. Period. While there may have been problems in your marriage that led to them going outside your relationship, they made the choice to have an affair instead of doing something more constructive to deal with those issues.

Trust in the process. Initially, the one who cheated is going to have to be willing to make amends, accept responsibility for what they've done and put in place boundaries to reassure you that they're not going to repeat their mistakes again.

Don't be afraid to get professional support to get you through this. You're both only human, and an objective outside counselor can help you maintain perspective and keep your focus on healing your relationship.

It will take time for you to be able to forgive your spouse. Don't rush yourself. It's crucial that any forgiveness is sincere and genuine. Otherwise, it could cause more problems in your relationship.

Look for ways you can rebuild intimacy between you. Don't feel that you have to rush into sex before you're ready but try at least to reach out physically with little gestures like holding hands or hugging. The more you can physically reconnect, the less likely you'll fall into the friend zone trap.

And remember why you're doing this. What is it about your marriage that makes you feel it's worth saving? Hold on to that reason and let it sustain you when the going gets tough.

In the introduction to this book, I told you about how I discovered my wife had an affair. It was the worst moment in my life. I didn't think we'd ever recover—but we did. I've learned to trust my wife again, and she goes out of her way to do those little things she knows mean so much to me. Our relationship is better than ever, and although it's been a few years since she cheated on me, we still go out of our way to practice many of the techniques I've given you in this book.

We actively make time to talk, and we're open and honest in our communication with each other. My wife gave me permission to check her phone whenever I liked, but I never did. Knowing she was willing to let me was all I needed to feel secure.

Betrayal is traumatic. It feels like part of you has died. But if your partner is open to change and you commit to the process, it's not too late to turn things around. As they say, "love is sweeter the second time around." If you're both determined to start fresh, you can rebuild what you've lost to enjoy a marriage even stronger than before. You can move forward together into a future filled with joy and contentment.

If you found this book useful, I'd love it if you could take a moment to leave a review. If you feel willing, you might even like to share how it's helped you recover from infidelity. A few words from you could help another couple discover this book and learn how to save their marriage too.

Finally, I want to wish you the very best of luck. I know what you're doing isn't easy, so please take time to acknowledge your strength and courage in making the decision to stay. I hope you find your way back to each other and enjoy many years of happiness together.

NOTES

INTRODUCTION

1. https://ifstudies.org/blog/who-cheats-more-the-demographics-of-cheating-in-america

1. UNDERSTANDING BETRAYAL

1. *Transcending Post-Infidelity Stress Disorder,* Dr. Dennis Ortman, 2009
2. https://fardapaper.ir/mohavaha/uploads/2021/06/Fardapaper-Coping-with-infidelity-The-moderating-role-of-self-esteem.pdf
3. https://www.frontiersin.org/articles/10.3389/fpsyg.2021.573123/full
4. Smith-Collins, A.P.R., Fiorentini, C., Kessler, E., Boyd, H., Roberts, F., & Skuse, D.H. (2012). Specific neural correlates of successful learning and adaptation during social exchanges. *Social, Cognitive, and Affective Neuroscience,* doi: 10.1093/scan/nss079
5. https://www.researchgate.net/publication/6781406_Romantic_Involvement_Often_Reduces_Men%27s_Testosterone_Levels-but_Not_Always_The_Moderating_Role_of_Extrapair_Sexual_Interest
6. https://pubmed.ncbi.nlm.nih.gov/28785917/

2. COMPLETE HONESTY

1. https://www.healthtestingcenters.com/research-guides/admitting-cheating/

Printed by Amazon Italia Logistica S.r.l.
Torrazza Piemonte (TO), Italy

59247535R00107